I0146439

Health
Ultimate Health Secrets

Strategies For Dieting, Eating Healthy, Exercising, Losing Weight, The Mediterranean Diet, Strength Training, And All About Vitamins, Minerals, And Supplements

By Ace McCloud
Copyright © 2014

Disclaimer

The information provided in this book is designed to provide helpful information on the subjects discussed. This book is not meant to be used, nor should it be used, to diagnose or treat any medical condition. For diagnosis or treatment of any medical problem, consult your own physician. The publisher and author are not responsible for any specific health or allergy needs that may require medical supervision and are not liable for any damages or negative consequences from any treatment, action, application or preparation, to any person reading or following the information in this book. Any references included are provided for informational purposes only. Readers should be aware that any websites or links listed in this book may change.

Table of Contents

Introduction 6

Chapter 1: The Benefits of Healthy Eating....................7

Chapter 2: Your Ultimate Guide to Dieting 10

Chapter 3: The Mediterranean Diet 22

Chapter 4: Coconut Oil and Skin Care........................27

Chapter 5: Protecting Your Body With Cardiovascular Exercise 32

Chapter 6: Strength Training 36

Chapter 7: Vitamins, Minerals, and Supplements 43

Chapter 8: Don't Forget Your Mental Health 54

Conclusion...57

My Other Books and Audio Books................................58

DEDICATED TO THOSE WHO ARE PLAYING THE GAME OF LIFE TO

WIN

KEEP ON PUSHING AND NEVER GIVE UP!

Ace McCloud

Be sure to check out my website for all my Books and Audio books.

www.AcesEbooks.com

Introduction

I want to thank you and congratulate you for buying the book, "Ultimate Health Secrets: Strategies For Dieting, Eating Healthy, Exercising, Losing Weight, The Mediterranean Diet, Strength Training, And All About Vitamins Minerals And Supplements."

This book contains proven steps and strategies on how to eat healthy, diet and exercise to look and feel your best! In the following pages you will discover everything that you need to know to be strong and healthy! Some of the things you will learn about include the best healthy foods to eat, how to create a customized diet plan for yourself, and how to create an exercise plan tailored towards your fitness goals. You will also discover cures to various ailments, anti-stress techniques, ways to boost your physical and mental energy, and most everything in between. You will also learn about the Mediterranean diet and the benefits of cooking with coconut oil for living your life at peak performance. This book is packed with delicious recipes, tips, strategies, secrets, visual aids, and tools that you can use to get you to the healthy body and energy levels desired! Stop wishing for health and vitality and start doing what really works! This book is your ultimate guide to living a happy and healthy life with a strong and energetic body.

Chapter 1: The Benefits of Healthy Eating

Eating is one thing that we all have in common—we eat to survive, we associate it with social functions (dinner parties, business meetings, birthdays, etc), and some people enjoy the art of preparing food. Eating is such an interesting and unique topic because it's so broad—there are so many types of foods that you can eat, there's so many ways prepare them, and there are foods that are good for you and foods that are bad. Our diets are important because they play a major role in our health. If you maintain a healthy diet and exercise, chances are that you will have good health. If you don't really watch what you eat or you don't exercise regularly, your health could probably use some help.

Another thing that many of us have in common is a limited amount of time. For many people, scheduling meals into their days is a real challenge. Many people fall into the habit of eating unhealthy foods because they are quick, easy, and readily available. However, most foods that you can easily pop into the microwave or eat right out of the package are filled with sugar, calories, trans fats, carbohydrates, high sodium levels, preservatives and other things that are bad for your body. They very rarely contain healthy minerals and nutrients. Although these kinds of foods are easy to eat and do not require much preparation, they come with many drawbacks.

Unhealthy foods can make us overweight and out of shape. They are also known to cause many diseases and conditions. Unfortunately, many corporations try to make their food as tasty and addictive as possible, worrying more about profits than the health of their customers. The most common disease that unhealthy foods can bring on is obesity. Obesity is a relevant and climbing problem in the United States. Studies suggest that at least 42% of our population will be obese by the year 2050—that's almost half of society! Doctors and researchers have linked obesity with other health complications such as heart disease and diabetes. Unhealthy eating can also lead to depression because your diet can affect your hormonal balance. The high sodium content in unhealthy foods can lead to kidney, liver, heart, and blood pressure complications. All in all, unhealthy eating can lead to nutritional deficiencies that can ultimately cause low energy, sleep problems, mood swings, and a hindered concentration. It is also easier to get injured with an unhealthy diet, it is easier to fall victim to sickness and it takes longer for your body to recover from these things.

It is important to eat healthy because good foods can provide your body with enough vitamins, minerals, and nutrients that it needs to function. By starting off on the right foot, you can avoid becoming obese and can avoid many unpleasant medical problems in the future. Healthy eating can make you feel upbeat, motivated, and energetic, which is important for living a fulfilling life. Healthy eating also pays off because it can strengthen your body against certain diseases, such as type 2 diabetes, heart disease, certain cancers, and heart disease. Healthy eating is essential for many aspects of our health and it sets a good example for your friends and family, especially the children in your life.

Healthy eating has many obvious benefits. It can help you control your weight and your appearance because you will not be consuming as much food that has a high fat and calorie count. Healthy foods can also fill you just as fast as unhealthy foods, so your chances of overeating may decrease. It can help you manage your blood sugar level and reduce your chances of developing type 2 diabetes because healthy foods do not contain as much sugar as traditional unhealthy foods. Healthy foods contain many antioxidants and low levels of cholesterol, which can help protect and strengthen your heart so that you can live a long, healthy life.

There are also some little-known benefits of eating healthy, which many people are not aware about. Eating healthy can help strengthen your teeth, fend off bad breath, reduce your chances of developing gum disease, reduce the amount of wrinkles on your skin, make you more productive, and it can keep your stress levels low. It can also prevent bloating, constipation, mood swings, and cravings. It can even make you more knowledgeable because it requires educating yourself to eat healthy. As you can see, there are more benefits to eating healthy than to eating unhealthy. It can positively affect almost every part of your body.

In a nutshell, think of this way: as long as you stay healthy, your chances of living longer and happier improve. You can live long enough to raise and support a family, you will save money by not having too many doctor visits, you can be happier, you can get more done, and people can look up to you as a healthy role model.

Some people confuse the idea of eating healthy as being on a diet. The truth is that eating healthy is not the same thing as being on a diet—people tend to only stay on diets for a certain amount of time—eating healthy is something that you should begin doing as soon as possible and you should continue to do it for the rest of your life.

This book is your ultimate guide to becoming and staying healthy in all areas of life. You will learn how to protect vulnerable parts of your body, such as your knees, back, and wrists. You will learn how to protect yourself against aging, cancers, vision problems, heart problems, anxiety, tension, and skin problems. You will learn how to become more confident, productive, energetic, and motivated to bring all the strategies in this book together in your life. I have been researching and writing about health, fitness, and self-improvement for some time now, and I am happy and excited to finally be able to share all of the best secrets, tips, and strategies with you.

When reading this book, keep this important tip in mind: change is hard and if you are currently living an unhealthy lifestyle, it won't be easy to change. However, you must remember that changes take time and patience. Do not allow the following chapters to overwhelm you or stress you out. Instead, take one step at a time until you are comfortable. Starting off slow is a good way to begin and work your way up to your goals. Take a few minutes to write out some health goals for yourself. Your goals can serve as your motivation as you plan to make some changes in your life. Make sure your goals have a powerful "**WHY**" that will truly motivate you to act consistently. For example, if you want to lose weight and gain strength... why do you want to do that? Is it so you can feel better about yourself? Is it so that you will be able to compete at a higher level? Is it because you want to be more attractive to the opposite sex? Is it so that you can live longer and happier with the people you love? Make sure your reason is compelling, something that truly motivates you, and remind yourself of it often. Most importantly, have fun! Changing your lifestyle in terms of health means that you get to try out new recipes, activities, and exercises, so have some fun with it and enjoy the process. Be sure to review your weight loss goals daily and use some visualization to see yourself in the healthy state of being that you want to be in.

Chapter 2: Your Ultimate Guide to Dieting

Many people think of dieting as a quick solution for becoming skinnier or healthier. However, a true diet is not so simple. A better way to define diet is the type and amount of food that you eat within a certain time frame. There are many different kinds of diets that you have probably heard of—the Atkins diet, the Zone diet, the Weight Watchers diet, the South Beach diet, the Raw Food diet, the Mediterranean diet, Paleo Diet, vegetarian diet, vegan diet, and more. These diets all use different strategies and theories to help people lose weight, but the one thing that they all have in common is that they aim to get people into the habit of eating balanced, nutritional meals.

A healthy diet is essentially a healthy lifestyle. The better you eat, the better your body can function. A healthy diet is one that includes food from each food group, since each group by itself cannot provide your body with the proper vitamins, minerals, and nutrients it needs to function. In this chapter, I will explain each food group so you have a better idea of the standard food pyramid. Then I will go over some great tips that you can follow as you start your own diet. You will also read about some very delicious yet healthy recipes you can start off with. Finally, I will talk about the importance of including exercise with your diet.

Best Foods to Eat for Dieting

You have probably heard about the food pyramid at one point in your life. Some packages of food have it on their labels but you have more likely learned about it in school. I don't know about you, but it's been a while since I've been a student, and it's easy to forget many of the things that you've learned in health class. I decided to include an overview of the major food groups so that you can refresh your memory and learn about what kind of foods are the best to eat while dieting.

Whole Grains

It is important for you to provide your body with at least 3 ounces of whole grains each day. Whole grains are better than refined grains (for example, wheat bread instead of white bread) because whole grains do not lose their bran and wheat germ when they are refined. Whole grains are an excellent source of fiber, vitamins, and minerals, which are essential for staying healthy and energetic. Most pastas, cereals, and bread come in whole grain options. You can also look for foods that contain 100% whole grains such as brown rice, corn, wild rice, and oatmeal. The best way to determine if something has whole grains in it is to carefully read the label.

Eating whole grains can help people whose stomachs do not respond well to acidic foods. At least 20% of the people in the United States suffer from a condition like this, which is better known as acid reflux. If you are susceptible to acid reflux and stomach pain, whole grain oatmeal is a great food to add to your diet. It contains plenty of vitamins, it slows down your digestion, and it is not acidic. You can have oatmeal for breakfast, you can incorporate it into breakfast smoothies, or you can have it topped off with fruits and nuts or ground cinnamon to help protect your body from even more ailments and conditions. Besides whole grains, you can also include honey, bananas, apples, ginger, and green tea in your diet. My personal favorite is Aloe Vera juice which has greatly helped with my own stomach problems. Four cups of Aloe Vera Juice a day, preferably 1 cup before each meal, 5 days a week with two days off per week can work wonders. Yoga is also the best type of exercise for those who experience acid reflux. For more detailed information on how to control acid reflux, please check out my book Acid Reflux Cure.

Fruits and Vegetables

It is important for you to provide your body with at least five servings of fruit and vegetables each day. They are generally great for you and can protect your body against a myriad of diseases and ailments. Fruits and vegetables are a very good source of nutrients. Studies also show that eating more fruits and vegetables can help protect you against heart disease, certain cancers, and type 2 diabetes. There are many ways to get your daily serving of fruits and vegetables. You can buy them fresh from the market, you can buy them frozen and use them in smoothies, or you can juice them into a delicious drink. Fruits and vegetables also have many great health benefits other than just protecting your body against diseases.

Red chili peppers have been found to be a good vegetable for suppressing your appetite because they contain a compound called Capsaicin. You can add these peppers to your eggs, your steak, your salads, or you can snack on them by themselves. Yellow bell peppers can help you burn more fat and contains three times the amount of vitamin C than oranges. Snacking on strawberries can help whiten your teeth due to their salicylic acid content. Adding beets to your salads can boost your endurance and make your muscles stronger.

Mangoes can help fend off breast cancer because of their polyphenolics, which can inhibit cancer cells. Adding sweet potatoes to your dinner plate can provide you with enough potassium to strengthen your muscles. The zinc in pumpkins and pumpkin seeds can help enhance your memory and hand-eye-coordination. Pineapples can help you reduce bloating because of their enzyme called bromelain, which is very helpful for digestion. The antioxidants found in corn can help protect your eyes and vision. Spinach can improve your complexion, pears can help you keep away hunger pains, and the healthy fats found in avocados can help you combat mood swings.

The natural acids found in plums can help you fend off a cold or virus. The flavonoids found in blueberries can help you focus, concentrate, and think logically. The simple sugars in raisins can give you a burst of natural energy and protect your bones from osteoporosis. The anti-inflammatory compounds found in onions can help protect your teeth against cavities and the high count of vitamin B6 in white potatoes can help lower your chances of developing heart disease.

If vision and eyesight problems run in your family or if you think that you are susceptible to them, some fruits and vegetables can help protect your eyes. Carrots, red onions, sweet potatoes broccoli, Brussels sprouts, spinach, and bell peppers all contain important vitamins and powerful antioxidants that can protect your eyes from cataracts and deterioration while promoting general eye health. Fruits that are good for promoting eye health include kiwi, cantaloupe, peaches, grapefruit, tomatoes, and oranges. Vision and eyesight problems can be hereditary so it is important to incorporate fruits and vegetables into your diet for extra protection. If you work in front of a computer or have a passion for video games, you can also eat plenty of fruits and vegetables to protect yourself from conditions such as glaucoma, myopia, hyberopia, cataracts, eye strain, and aging. If you would learn all the tips, exercises, and secrets for protecting and enhancing your eyesight, please check out my book Eyesight and Vision Cure.

There are many more types of fruits and vegetables that you can add to your diet, but this chapter should give you a good idea of just how important they are to your overall health. Fruits and vegetables are delicious, filling, refreshing, and versatile—you can become very creative when it comes to cooking with these two foods, so you will not have to worry about getting tired of eating them.

You can also get your daily servings of fruits and vegetables by making smoothies. Smoothies are quick and easy to make and you can have them as a meal or as a snack. You are probably familiar with fruit smoothies but did you know that you can even make vegetable smoothies? They are better known as green smoothies. There is an unlimited variety of smoothies you can make, so feel free to mix and match your favorite fruits and vegetables. Here are a few recipes you can try out:

Strawberry Yogurt Smoothie

Combine 4 cups of strawberries, 1 cup of yogurt, 1 orange, and a tablespoon of honey together and then blend for 60 seconds or until smooth.

General Green Smoothie Recipe

- 1-2 Cups of leafy greens, preferably kale, spinach, collards or chard.
- 2 fruits: For example, 1 banana and 1 apple.
- 1 vegetable such as a cucumber, carrot or celery.
- 1-2 Cups Liquid. Water, Milks, Fruit Juices. The amount will depend on how much you want in your smoothie and how much it takes to blend in the fruits and vegetables. It is generally best to use water in the vast majority of healthy smoothies.

Spinach, Avocado, and Apple Smoothie

Combine one and a half cup of apple juice, two cups of spinach, one chopped apple, and the chopped pieces of half an avocado. Blend until smooth.

Spinach, Grape, and Coconut Smoothie

Combine half a cup of ice, one cup of green grapes, one cup of spinach, and a quarter cup of coconut milk and blend together until smooth.

Meat, Poultry, Fish, Nuts and Eggs

Meat, poultry, fish, and eggs are very important for your body because these foods all contain protein. Protein helps your body build and repair tissue. These foods also contain important nutrients such as zinc, iron, magnesium, and B vitamins. Health experts recommend that 25% of your diet should include protein-rich foods. When eating meat, be sure to trim it of all its fat and you can optionally take the skin off of the chicken before eating it. I also recommend eating fish at least twice a week because it contains omega-3 fatty acids, which are also beneficial to your health. The best way to eat meat, chicken, and fish is to grill or roast it. Frying it is another option but fried foods are not as good for your health.

Avoiding Constipation

Nuts and seeds can be especially helpful in protecting your insides from constipation, a condition that nobody wants to experience, and nuts and seeds are also great for energy. The older you get, the more constipation can be a problem, so it is very important to watch what you eat. Flax seeds in particular are helpful with this condition because of their high fiber content. Almonds, sunflower seeds, and sesame seeds can also serve as a solution to constipation. Try to avoid red meats, dairy, caffeine, processed foods, and sugar, as all these foods can worsen constipation. It is also important to eat a balanced and healthy diet, especially if you have diabetes, which worsen constipation. Prune juice is also an incredible all natural solution and drinking lots of water, smoothies, and fruit and vegetable juices helps tremendously as well. Constipation medicine can get pretty pricey so it can be helpful to turn to alternative solutions. For a more in-depth look at constipation and how it affects your body, please check out my book Constipation Cure.

Milk, Yogurt, and Cheese

Milk, yogurt, and cheese fall in the category of dairy products. Eating dairy products is a great way to provide your body with calcium and it makes your bones and teeth strong. For the best results, you should try to stick with low-fat dairy products. Vegans can get their sources of calcium through vegetables such as broccoli or cabbage or through vitamin supplements.

Kidney Stones

Adding the proper amount of calcium to your diet can protect your body against kidney stones, which is another horrible and very painful condition that nobody wants to experience. Many people end up in the hospital from kidney stones and those who have had them many times describe it as the worst pain that they have ever experienced. If you are prone to dehydration, if you are overweight, addicted to alcohol, adding salt to all of your food, or eating foods that contain high fructose corn syrup, you may be more susceptible to kidney stones. Too much calcium can also cause kidney stones but on the other hand, if you don't provide your body with *enough* calcium, you may still be at risk. Low fat milk and low fat cheese are two great, calcium-rich foods that you can add to your diet to help fend off kidney stones. Drinking lots of water is also a great way to avoid getting kidney stones. For a more in-depth look at kidney stones, please check out my book Kidney Stones Cure.

Fats and Sugars

Products with high amounts of sugar and fat, such as butter, chocolate, sodas, mayonnaise, cakes, and a variety of other processed foods should only be eaten sparingly. Products that contain high levels of saturated fats, such as cream, margarine, and fried foods should especially be kept to a minimum; although some saturated fats like the ones found in coconut oil can be very good for you (discussed in more detail in chapter 4).

You don't have to completely torture yourself and cut fats and sugars out of your diet forever, but you should try to limit them from your diet. By limiting these types of foods, they will taste even better when you do allow yourself to have them.

Acne

Not only can an excess of sugars lead to obesity, it can also lead to skin problems such as acne. Acne is a breakout on the skin that affects people of all ages. **To control acne, it is very important to eat right.** Certain foods can trigger the production of hormones and oil (sugar being one of them), while others can promote good skin health (such as vegetables, fruits, and nuts). Acne is not a life-threatening condition but it can make you look unattractive or feel unpleasant. To get rid of it, you can turn to special facial cleaners, acne creams, laser treatment, or a variety of modern medicines, all of which can be costly. Good "food treatments" for clearing up acne include using grapes, cucumbers, honey, lemons and orange peels as all natural facial cleansers because of their antibacterial, acidic, and moisturizing properties. For more information on how to treat acne naturally and for some excellent recipes to combat acne, please check out my book Acne Cure.

Creating the Ultimate Diet Plan

To be able to diet properly, I highly recommend having a plan. Creating a personalized diet plan can help you better address your eating preferences while working around your school or work schedule. It can also serve as a visual or a map, which can make your diet easier to follow.

The first thing you should do when creating a personalized diet plan is reflect upon yourself. The better you know yourself, the better you can figure out what kind of diet plan you need in order to see successful results. There are a couple of basic, key questions that you can ask yourself to start out.

First, ask yourself how many meals you would like to eat per day. Some people can get away with eating two meals but others may like to break their meals up. I would highly recommend breaking your meals up into smaller portions and eating 4-5 times per day. Once I started breaking up my meals into smaller, healthier portions is when I noticed a tremendous increase in my overall wellbeing.

When you've figured out how many meals you want to eat per day, you can try to divide the total amount of calories you want to consume each day by the number of meals that you eat each day. **For example, if you only want to eat 2,000 calories per day, you can eat 4 meals of 500 calorie or 2 meals of 1,000 calories, or any combination.** Here is one tip: you should try to eat at least three meals per day. Eating smaller meals consistently can help prevent overeating and increase overall alertness and energy level. If you are doing strength training and regular exercise, you often times do not even have to count calories, just eat healthy and when your hungry. Over time this strategy tends to lead towards an athletic and strong body that is not over weight.

Secondly, ask yourself how much time you will be able to spend preparing your meals. If you're not a fan of cooking or if you have a busy schedule, you will have to figure out how you're going to coordinate your meal preparation. This will all depend on your own schedule. For example, it might be better for you to prepare all of your meals in advance on Sunday night and keep them in your refrigerator/freezer. This strategy can save you lots of time compared to preparing a fresh meal each night.

Thirdly, take a minute to reflect on your support system. To be successful at anything, having a strong and encouraging support system can help you reach your goals. You can ask your family and friends if they would like to diet with you, which can help make the process easier. If they do not want to diet with you, ask them to be supportive of your decision. You might even want to find somebody else who is dieting, eating healthy, or in being a workout buddy to help keep you motivated.

Fourthly, if you know you're going to eat out at a restaurant, try to find out what their menu is like beforehand. Make sure you take into account everything that you eat and try to pick out the healthiest options. You can even stick to your diet when eating out by making simple swaps, such as getting fresh vegetables instead of fries or skipping out on the free bread.

Fifthly, don't leave your sweet tooth in the dust. Being on a diet does not mean that you have to cut out tasty treats completely; it just means that you have to be more aware of what and how much you eat. If you tend to crave junk food, make room for it in your diet so that you don't binge on it later. A good idea is to set aside 100 calories in your diet for when you're having a junk food craving. Chocolate is always a favorite, and dark chocolate is actually healthy for you. Just choose something that you like as a reward for all your hard work

The best part about creating a personal diet plan is that you get to choose what kinds of foods you want to eat every day. As you begin to create your own diet plan, think about the different kinds of foods you can include from each food group. When planning out your meals, take these few tips into consideration:

- You can stay full by combining protein and fiber. Your body will feel more satisfied from having a lunch that consists of a piece of fruit, a yogurt cup, and a cooked egg rather than a bag of chips and a soda. A really great, easy lunch that has worked out for me is combining four tablespoons of low-fat, vanilla yogurt with a bowl of pumpkin flavored granola. It keeps me full between breakfast and dinner and it's very healthy and tasty. I like vanilla and pumpkin flavors, but you can use any combination of yogurt and granola flavors to switch it up.

- When going grocery shopping, try to opt for the low-fat options if they're available. For example, pick skim milk over whole milk and 93% ground beef over 73% ground beef. Also try to stick to natural foods instead of processed foods. For example, switching low-fat milk for whole milk can be effective because your body will still get calcium. You can also switch to Almond Milk, which is one of my favorites! It stays fresh for months at a time, tastes great, is healthy, and can be substituted for milk products quite easily.

- Invest in a small kitchen scale and measuring cup set to help measure your meal proportions. Even though you can pretty much eat all the fruits and vegetables that you want without harming your body, it is easy to go overboard on things like cheese, meat, and pasta.

When creating a diet plan, a good idea is to create your own menu. You can research recipes and figure out what works best for you but by having an idea of what you're going to eat ahead of time. You can save yourself time, money, and health by planning ahead and making great eating choices. Here is an example of a diet plan menu for a person who is planning on eating four meals per day (breakfast, lunch, dinner, and snack):

Breakfast: Strawberry Oatmeal Breakfast Smoothie

This breakfast recipe is great for dieting because it's simple and easy to make, takes only 5 minutes, and has an excellent nutritional value. This smoothie contains a little over 10% of the calories allotted for a 2,000 calorie diet and does not have a high fat content.

You will need:

- 1 cup of soy or almond milk
- ½ cup of rolled oats
- 1 banana, broken into pieces
- 14 strawberries, frozen
- ½ teaspoon of vanilla extract
- 1 ½ teaspoons of white sugar

Combine the soy milk, oats, banana pieces, and strawberries in a blender and blend until smooth. You can optionally add the vanilla and sugar. Pour the mixture into a glass and enjoy.

Lunch: Bean Quesadillas

What's a more fun lunch option than healthy quesadillas? Quesadillas are delicious, easy to make, and portable, so you can make them at home and bring them along with you to work or school. This recipe takes less than an hour to make and has a lot of protein and fiber.

You will need:

- 1 tablespoon of vegetable oil
- 1 onion, diced
- 2 cloves of garlic, minced
- 1 can of black beans, drained
- 1 green pepper, chopped
- 2 tomatoes, chopped
- ½ a package of frozen corn
- 12 12-inch flour tortillas
- 1 cup of shredded cheddar cheese
- ¼ cup of vegetable oil

In a pan over medium heat, heat one tablespoon of vegetable oil and cook the onion and garlic until they are soft. Add the beans, green pepper, tomatoes, and corn and cook until the mixture is well heated. Add the vegetable mixture to 6 flat tortillas and add the shredded cheese. Top the tortillas with the other 6 ingredients to create the actual quesadilla. In another pan, add the ¼ cup of vegetable oil over medium-high heat and then cook each quesadilla until the cheese melts and each side is lightly browned.

Dinner: Sweet and Hot Glazed Salmon

This recipe makes a great dinner dish and features one of the healthiest kinds of fish. It takes less than an hour to make, which makes it a great option for those with busy schedules. This recipe contains a little over 10% of the allotted calories of a 2,000 calorie diet and it has a high protein count.

You will need:

- 1 and a half cups of apricot nectar
- 1/4 cup of dried, chopped apricots
- 2 tablespoons of honey
- 2 tablespoons of reduced sodium soy salt
- 1 tablespoon of grated ginger
- Minced garlic
- 1/8 teaspoon of cayenne pepper
- ¼ teaspoon of ground cinnamon
- 2 lbs of skinless salmon filet

Preheat your oven and grease a pain. In the pan over medium heat, combine the apricot nectar, dried apricots, soy sauce, honey, garlic, ginger, cayenne, and cinnamon. Allow the mixture to start boiling and then let it simmer for 20 minutes. Stir the mixture occasionally so that it does not burn. Take out ¼ cup of the mixture for basting and put the rest aside. Place the salmon on the greased pan and cover it with the mixture that you just took out. Broil the salmon for 12 minutes or until it flakes. Turn it over as it cooks and baste it during the last 4 minutes of cooking. Serve it with the leftover glaze for extra flavor.

Snack: Whole Wheat Strawberry Banana Muffins

If you're a fan of strawberry banana-flavored foods, you're going to love these whole wheat strawberry banana muffins. These muffins make for a great snack at home or on the go and they only take approximately a half-hour to make. With a low calorie and fat count, they are a mouth-watering, great-tasting snack and much better than candy, chips, cookies, or any other traditional snacks.

You will need:

- 2 eggs
- Half a cup of unsweetened applesauce
- A quarter cup of vegetable oil
- ¾ cup of brown sugar
- 1 teaspoon of vanilla extract

- 3 bananas
- Two cups of whole wheat flour
- 1 teaspoon of baking soda
- 1 tablespoon of ground cinnamon
- 1 and a half cups of strawberries

Preheat your oven to 375 degrees and get a muffin pan ready. In a bowl, mix the applesauce, eggs, brown sugar, oil, bananas and vanilla together. In a separate bowl, add the flour, baking soda, and cinnamon together and stir. Next, add the flour mixture to the banana mixture and stir in the strawberries. Once everything is combined together, spoon it into the muffin pan. Bake for 20 minutes and let it cool before removing.

Considering Vegetarianism

One great way to stay healthy and lose weight is to consider vegetarianism. Vegetarians do not eat meat but many will still eat eggs and dairy. In fact, just being a vegetarian can decrease your overall chances of being obese, developing various diseases and cancers, and it can help you live longer. Vegetarianism is great for those who love to eat a lot but don't want to put on too much weight. It can also help you save money, since meat tends to be pretty expensive. You don't even have to commit to being a vegetarian full time, just adding a few days a week of a vegetarian diet has proven to have incredible health benefits. If you are really interested in some great, easy, and delicious vegetarian recipes, please check out my book Vegetarian Diet, Recipes, and Cooking, where you can learn more about the benefits of vegetarianism and get a lot of incredible food recipes.

Finding the Time to Prepare Meals

One factor that often holds many people back from preparing their own meals is time. While it is true that time is limited for many people who work, support their families, and have other obligations, it is very possible to make time for meal planning and preparation. One way to make time for this is to figure out how to become more productive. By making simple changes in your life, you can accrue extra time that you didn't even know you had to get more done. Everybody's productivity strategy will be different, but for an in-depth guide on how to fit meal preparation and more into your life, please check out my book Ultimate Productivity, where you can learn about different time management strategies, habits, and techniques for a more positive, productive and fulfilling life. Being more productive also makes it easier to find the time to exercise!

Incorporating Exercise Into Your Diet Plan

Speaking of exercise, it is important to remember that a diet plan will generally not work unless you're exercising at the same time. Exercising while you are dieting is very important because it helps your body burn fat. It also makes your bones, muscles, joints, lungs, and other important body parts healthy and strong.

Many people make the mistake of thinking that they can eat badly and then "exercise it off." In reality, junk food is so horrible for your body that it can take hours and hours of exercise just to burn it off, that is if you can find the energy to do so after such poor eating choices. By eating healthy in the first place, you can lose weight quicker, keep it off, and your overall health and energy levels will be much better.

The best types of exercises to engage in while dieting are cardio and strength training. We will go much deeper into these subjects in the next couple of chapters. In a nutshell, cardio helps you improve the way your lungs and heart function and strength training helps build your strength, muscles and metabolism. Dieting alone can tend to make your metabolism slow down, so exercising regularly can help keep it up. The best way to get into the habit of exercising while dieting is to form a regular exercise routine.

It is important to remember that you should start out slow when you're first starting out. Don't try to go crazy on your first day of exercising, otherwise you will most likely tire yourself out, get injured, or be so sore the next day that you won't want to stick with it. If you're new to exercise, start out with something easy, like walking, and work your way up to cardio and strength training exercises.

A good way to know when to step up your training program is when you've gotten comfortable doing one type of exercise. Look at it as a challenge—when you've gotten used to walking, maybe try jogging, and then upgrade to running. You may be sore after the first couple rounds of exercising but as long as you stay consistent, there is a good chance that you will feel so great that you won't want to stop exercising. I get exercise into my schedule each day. I started out slow by stretching and warming up, and then gradually build up the intensity. It is generally best, on a strength training day, to do the strength training first and then the cardio for optimal results.

Staying Motivated While Dieting

Dieting is not easy because it involves changing your lifestyle and many people are afraid of change. However, not all change is bad, especially if you are changing your diet because you're probably changing it for the better. By establishing a solid foundation of self-discipline and willpower for yourself, while incorporating a good strategy, can make the change to a better diet much easier. Did you know that making healthy choices can even help you enhance your willpower?

Studies have shown that people with low levels of blood glucose levels have a harder time mastering willpower than those who have higher levels. You do not want your blood glucose level to become too high, however, as you may put yourself at risk for developing diabetes. You can help strengthen your willpower by maintaining a healthy level of blood glucose in your body. By cutting out junk food and anything else that contains sugar, you can help level out your blood glucose levels and consequently you will boost your willpower and health at the same time.

Also, adding plenty of wheat and whole-grain options to your diet can help enhance your willpower, as well. Many grocery stores offer whole-grain options in breads, pastas, and more so always go for the better kind. You'll be doing your body a favor and over time, you may find it easier to control your cravings. Fruits and vegetables are also helpful for fueling your body properly. When it comes to exercising your willpower, think of it this way: it is just like any other muscle in your body—the more you use it, the stronger it will be.

Practicing self-discipline is also essential when it comes to dieting and living a healthy lifestyle. Obviously, it takes a lot of self-discipline to pass over junk food or to get up off the couch and exercise. Self-Discipline is often fueled by willpower, so as long as you focus on eating right, it shouldn't be too hard to get into the habit.

One good way to start practicing self-discipline in your everyday life is to make one change at a time. For example, when it comes to changing your diet, don't dive headfirst into making a million changes at once. For example, I started out by switching out white bread for whole-grain bread and then I started switching whole milk for Almond milk, and so on. I got used to eating healthier much quicker than I expected. It is a little like working your way up the exercise ladder. Like dieting, another good way to practice strengthening your self-discipline is to make a plan and stick to it.

Finally, do not be discouraged if you take a step backward. Nobody is perfect and we all have given into temptation at some point in our lives. The key is to just reflect upon your mistakes and then work to solve them next time. Having willpower and self-discipline can help make dieting much easier and it can also help you out in other areas of your life, such as handling money, your relationships, your working life and resisting the temptation to abuse harmful substances. For a more in-depth look at how to master willpower and self-discipline, you can check out my other book, Influence, Willpower, and Discipline to learn how to increase your influence over yourself and others, how to practice building your willpower, and how to improve your self-discipline to get the most successful results out of your life. Once you've mastered all of this, then you really can bring out the best in yourself and your life.

Chapter 3: The Mediterranean Diet

The Mediterranean diet is a diet that favors fruits, vegetables, and nuts over foods such as red meats, saturated fats and sugars. Some people do not even like to call it a diet—they see it more as a lifestyle. It is named after the people who live near the Mediterranean Sea, who tend to have lives that are long and healthy. Those on a Mediterranean diet tend to have less heart issues and a lower rate of cancer development. Many experts believe that people who live near the Mediterranean Sea are healthier because of their diet and active lifestyle. The Mediterranean diet has been designed to mimic the diet of these people. There have been many studies that have found the Mediterranean diet to be one of the healthiest diets in the world.

One great thing about the Mediterranean diet is that it is not structured from one culture—it is a diet that has many common values from many cultures. Since Greeks, Italians, French, and Spanish people all eat different kinds and styles of food; no dish is ever the same. Instead, the Mediterranean diet is a generalized pattern of eating. A basic Mediterranean diet food pyramid includes the categories of fruits and vegetables, whole grains, nuts, legumes, beans, spices, olive oil, herbs, and seafood. The pyramid suggests that yogurt, cheese, poultry, and eggs should be eaten in moderation and red meat and sugar should be saved for once in a while. It also suggests adding a glass of red wine to your meals, which has been proven to fend off heart disease in regular drinkers. It doesn't just have to be red wine, however. Recent studies have shown that a small amount of just about any type of alcohol can have the same beneficial effects.

Whole grains are encouraged in the Mediterranean diet because they are not processed, meaning they still contain many of the valuable nutrients that your body needs, like fiber and vitamins. Common grains that qualify for the Mediterranean diet include buckwheat, barley, rice, oats, breads, and pasta. You can often easily switch out white bread and regular pasta for whole-grain versions. They are very easy to find in your local grocery store.

Vegetables are a primary food in the Mediterranean diet because they contain plenty of nutrients and they are filling. You can eat them raw or you can cook them and top them off with a little olive oil. Common vegetables that qualify for the Mediterranean diet include artichokes, Brussels sprouts, celery, cabbage, carrots, cucumbers, collard greens, kale, eggplant, mushrooms, lettuce, lemons, onions, peppers, okra, peas, radishes, potatoes, pumpkins, sweet potatoes, scallions, zucchini, and spinach.

Fruits, like vegetables, are also a primary food group in the Mediterranean diet because of their nutritional benefits. Common fruits that qualify for the Mediterranean diet include avocados, apples, clementines, cherries, apricots, grapefruits, dates, figs, melons, nectarines, grapes, pears, oranges, peaches, tomatoes, strawberries, pomegranates, and pears.

Another category of food in the Mediterranean diet is nuts, beans, and legumes. These foods are important because they are good sources of fiber, protein, and good fats. Common foods in this category include chickpeas, almonds, cashews, green beans, lentils, kidney beans, sesame seeds, pistachios, walnuts, and tahini sauce.

The two most common types of drinks in the Mediterranean diet are water and wine. Water helps you stay hydrated, has zero calories, and helps boost your levels of energy. It is a better alternative to sugary drinks. Red wine is also popular in the Mediterranean diet because it is known to have positive effects on your health. Of course, you should only drink wine in moderation. The standard serving for men is two five ounce glasses per day and one five ounce glass per day for women.

One thing that makes the Mediterranean diet very unique is that it replaces butter, salad dressings, and other fats used for baking and cooking. The best type of olive oil to use is extra virgin. You can also still eat yogurt and cheese if you're trying out the Mediterranean diet, but it is important to limit these products.

Which Pyramid is Better?

The Mediterranean Diet can serve as a good strategy for controlling diabetes, if you have it, and it can help prevent it, if you don't. Since one of the primary risk factors for developing type 2 diabetes is being overweight, following the Mediterranean diet can help you fend it off since it helps you stay fit. It is also a diet that is safe for adults, children, and the elderly. No matter how old you are, you can safely get into a better lifestyle by following the Mediterranean diet. It is also easy to adapt gluten-free, low salt, and Kosher diets to the Mediterranean diet.

Finally, don't be worried about having to eat bland food. Sacrificing foods that are high in sugar, fat, and cholesterol does not mean that you have to sacrifice taste. Almost every dish that can be made with foods from the Mediterranean diet is flavorful and savory. Sometimes you will even feel like you are eating out instead of eating at home.

Mediterranean Diet Factors

The Mediterranean diet is not only healthy because of the kinds of foods it promotes—there are some other factors that contribute to good health and a long life expectancy. Mediterranean people are also well-known for sharing their meals, appreciating health, and exercising daily.

For the Mediterranean diet to be successful, you must incorporate plenty of exercise into your life. Although walking is big in the Mediterranean region, you can do any kind of exercise, as long as you keep yourself moving. For the best results, you should try to plan an exercise regimen that contains at least 30 minutes of a moderately intense cardio exercise at least four times a week, while also following a strength training routine that covers all of the major body parts in one week.

The Best and Healthiest Mediterranean Diet Recipes

Black Bean Hummus

Black bean hummus makes for a great and healthy snack, anywhere or anytime. It's also very simple and easy to make—it only takes 5 minutes to prepare and it has a low calorie count.

You will need:

- 1 garlic clove
- ½ teaspoon of salt
- 1 15 oz can of black beans (drain and reserve juice)
- ¼ teaspoon cayenne pepper
- 2 tablespoons of lemon juice
- ¼ teaspoon paprika
- 1 ½ tablespoons of tahini
- 10 Greek olives
- ¾ teaspoon of ground cumin

Use a food processor to mince the garlic. Add the beans, 2 tablespoons of the bean juice, the lemon juice, the tahini, the cumin, the salt, and the cayenne pepper and process the mixture until it is smooth. Top it off with paprika and Greek olives and use it as a dip for pita bread or delicious raw vegetables.

Greek Penne and Chicken

Greek penne and chicken is a delicious and healthy dish that serves as a great dinner. Though this recipe has a higher calorie count than usual, its protein count is tremendous.

You will need:

- 1 box of penne noodles
- 1 and 1/3 tablespoons of butter
- A red onion, chopped
- Minced garlic
- 2 lbs of skinless, boneless chicken
- 1 can of artichoke hearts in water
- 1 tomato, chopped
- Half a cup of crumbled feta
- 2 tablespoons of parley

- 2 tablespoons of lemon juice
- 1 and a half teaspoons of oregano

Boil the penne in water until it is softened. Drain the pasta when it's done cooking. While the pasta is cooking, melt some butter in a skillet over medium to high heat. Add the onion and garlic to the skillet and cook the mixture for 2 minutes. Then add the pieces of chicken and continue to cook until they are golden brown, occasionally stirring for 5 minutes. Reduce the heat to medium-low and drain the artichokes. Add the artichokes along with the tomato, feta cheese, parsley, lemon juice, oregano, and penne. Cook it all until it's hot. Season the dish with salt and pepper and then serve.

Greek Lentil Soup

Greek lentil soup is an excellent, Mediterranean-diet friendly and an easy-to-make dish for anytime of the day. Unlike the first two dishes, this one takes a little longer to make, but its taste and healthy properties are well worth the effort. With a moderate calorie count and fat content, this soup is an excellent dish.

You will need:

- 8 ozs of brown lentils
- ¼ cup of olive oil
- 1 tablespoon of minced garlic
- 1 minced onion
- 1 large chopped carrot
- 1 quart of water
- 1 pinch of dried oregano
- 1 pinch of dried rosemary
- 2 bay leaves
- 1 tablespoon of tomato paste
- Salt and pepper to taste
- 1 teaspoon of olive oil to taste
- 1 teaspoon of red wine vinegar to taste

Fill a pan with an inch of water and the lentils. Over high heat, boil the water and allow the lentils to cook for 10 minutes. Then drain the lentils with a strainer. Dry out the saucepan and add ¼ cup of olive oil over medium heat. Add the garlic, onion, and carrots and stir the mixture for 5 minutes. Next, pour in the lentils, 1 quart of water, the spices, and the bay leaves. Bring it to a boil. Reduce the heat to medium-low, cover the saucepan, and simmer the mixture for 10 minutes. Next, stir in the tomato paste and add salt and pepper if you wish. Cover it again and simmer for 30 to 40 minutes while occasionally stirring. If the soup becomes too thick, you can add water. When it's ready, drizzle it with olive oil or red wine vinegar.

Mediterranean Breakfast Quinoa

This delicious breakfast dish utilizes quinoa, which many people regard as a "super-food" for its extra healthy properties. You can enjoy this dish in the morning for breakfast or at any time of the day, since it only takes 25 minutes to make. This recipe has a moderate calorie count and a high level of protein.

You will need:

- 1 cup of raw almonds, chopped
- 1 teaspoon of ground cinnamon
- 1 cup of quinoa
- 2 cups of milk
- 1 teaspoon of sea salt
- 1 teaspoon of vanilla extract
- 2 tablespoons of honey
- 2 dates, dried, pitted and finely chopped
- 5 apricots, dried and finely chopped

Over medium heat, toast the almonds for 3 to 5 minutes and set them aside. In another saucepan, heat the quinoa and cinnamon over medium heat until the mixture is warmed through. Stir in the milk and the sea salt. Allow it to boil and then simmer for 15 minutes. Next, stir in the vanilla, dates, honey, almonds, and apricots. If you have any leftover almonds, you can top the oatmeal off with them.

Chapter 4: Coconut Oil and Skin Care

Coconut Oil

Coconut oil has recently been hailed as an extremely healthy super food. People have been cooking with coconut oil since the 19th century, although originally, many people were turned away from it because of its high content of saturated fat.

At that time, many people were under the misconception that saturated fats could lead to heart disease, high cholesterol, and other unhealthy ailments. Nowadays, however, it is viewed as a very healthy oil that can be eaten raw or used in cooking. It also has no known links to heart disease. You should still, however, watch how much saturated fat you consume. Proof that coconut oil is healthy for you has come from the diets of those who live in tropical climates. The diets of these people contain high amounts of coconut oil and they tend to have much less heart and health problems than other people in typical western diets. Coconut oil is now accepted as a healthy option.

There are two primary types of coconut oil: virgin or extra virgin and refined or expeller-pressed. Virgin coconut oil contains more antioxidants as well as a stronger coconut taste and smell. Refined coconut oil has less of a strong coconut taste and it is better for cooking in high heat. Both types tend to have an unrefrigerated shelf life of about two years.

Coconut oil is usually solid at room temperature, so you will have to melt it down before you can use it to cook. The best way to melt it down is to place it in a microwave-safe bowl and heat it up for a few seconds. You can also melt it by placing it in a bowl with very hot water. It makes a great substitute for butter and you can use it to give a little jazz to foods such as homemade granola, roasted vegetables, and pastries. You can even use it to pop popcorn or to make your own mayonnaise.

The Benefits of Cooking with Coconut Oil

So what sets coconut oil apart from vegetable oil, canola oil, or some other kind of cooking oil? First and foremost, it contains about 90% of saturated fats. The good part about this is that it makes coconut oil resistant to oxidation when exposed to high heat, making it a great oil to fry foods with. Coconut oil also contains a set of fatty acids that your body can quickly and easily turn into energy. It also contains a fatty acid that can help protect your body from infections caused by bacteria and viruses. Additionally, it can help improve your levels of "good" cholesterol, it can help people who have Alzheimer's disease, and it can reduce your chances of having a seizure.

You can use coconut oil as a mouthwash to reduce bad breath and to strengthen your teeth. Interestingly enough, you can also use coconut oil as a bug repellent, deodorant, dandruff relief, makeup remover, lip balm, butter substitute, and even as a coffee creamer! It can even serve as a great supplement for anti-aging. Coconut oil can protect your hair and skin from being damaged and it can even serve as a sunscreen.

Losing Weight With Coconut Oil

Studies have recently found that coconut oil can help you lose weight in comparison with using soybean oil. One reason for this is that coconut oil can make you feel fuller and it can also increase your energy levels, which can lead you to become more active. Coconut oil is also especially useful for getting rid of abdominal fat, which is the most dangerous type of fat because it can lead to several different types of diseases. Studies show that coconut oil can effectively help both genders lose weight.

Easy and Healthy Coconut Oil Recipes

Homemade Mayonnaise

I mentioned earlier that you can use coconut oil to make your own mayonnaise, which is a great idea because store-bought mayonnaise contains trans-fats. If you love to spread mayonnaise on your sandwiches but you are concerned about your diet, learning how to make homemade mayonnaise with coconut oil can be an easy, quick fix. This recipe utilizes coconut oil and olive oil, so you will be using two of the healthiest oils.

You will need:

- 1 egg
- 2 yolks
- 1 tablespoon of mustard
- 1 tablespoon of lemon juice
- ½ teaspoon of salt
- ¼ teaspoon of pepper
- ½ cup of virgin coconut oil
- ½ cup of virgin olive oil
- Patience

Combine all ingredients except the oils and blend for a few seconds. Run your blender on the lowest speed available and then begin to add the oils, but very slowly. Start out by dripping it into the blender and then only let it pour out in a very small stream. This process should take at least 5 minutes.

Coconut Oil Italian Dressing

This recipe will allow you to create a healthy, homemade salad dressing that is much healthier than the kind you can buy at the store. Like the mayonnaise recipe, this one also utilizes both types of healthy oil. When you pour it over your salad, you will only be making it healthier and yummier!

You will need:

- ¼ cup of coconut water vinegar
- 2 tablespoons of water
- ½ cup of coconut oil
- ½ cup of olive oil
- 1 teaspoon of salt
- 1 teaspoon of Italian seasoning

Simply whisk all of these ingredients together to create an excellent salad dressing. You can store any leftover dressing in the refrigerator, as it will stay in liquid form.

Chocolate Mint Fudge

Coconut oil can even make dessert healthy. This fun recipe takes less than 10 minutes to make. It is a great way to factor dessert into your diet and it is much healthier than eating a piece of cake. If you work hard on sticking to your diet and exercise routine, go ahead and reward yourself with this recipe. It doesn't come out very sweet but you can still get a taste of chocolate.

You will need:

- ½ cup of coconut oil
- ¼ cup of softened, grass-fed butter
- ¼ cup of raw cocoa powder
- ¼ cup of raw honey
- 1 tablespoon of vanilla extract
- 5 drops of mint extract

Use a mixing cup in hot water to melt your coconut oil. Once melted, add the rest of the ingredients to the oil and mix together while keeping the cup in hot water. Take the cup out of the water and use a blender to thoroughly mix the ingredients. Next, pour the mixture into a candy mold and put it in the refrigerator. Allow it to harden and then enjoy.

Best Kinds of Coconut Oil

If you're looking to buy extra virgin coconut oil, you can't go wrong with Viva Labs Organic Coconut Oil. For a reasonable price, this container comes with 16 ounces of oil. It is organic, kosher, and gluten free. It also does not contain any trans-fats, GMOs, bleach, or pesticides. It is excellent for losing weight and becoming more energized. You can use this oil for cooking, as a dietary supplement, or as a skin and hair care product.

If you're looking to buy a refined coconut oil, check out Spectrum Refined Organic Coconut Oil. This package comes with two jars of organic, kosher oil for a reasonable price. This oil does not have a strong coconut flavor or taste and is good for cooking and moisturizing your skin. This product is also especially good for hair care.

Skin Care

There are several other things that you can use for all-natural skin moisturizing besides coconut oil. You can use buttermilk, honey, avocado, green tea, ginger tea, and even olive oil to help yourself stay young-looking.

Buttermilk contains lactic acid, one of the acids that can decrease the amount of dead skin cells retained by your skin. Rinse a towel in buttermilk and put it on your face. Then, rinse gently with warm water so that some of the lactic acid remains on your skin. Honey is a natural humectant. This means that it draws moisture from the air. If you mix equal parts honey and water, then apply it to your skin, the same effect occurs: the water is drawn to and absorbed by your skin, thereby moisturizing it. After 15 minutes, rinse it off.

A mashed avocado also makes a very good moisturizer. The avocado oils are a natural emollient that lubricates the spaces between your skin cells. Furthermore, these oils are readily absorbed by the skin increasing elasticity and giving a smooth appearance. The vitamins contained in avocados also help your skin get rid of dead cells and helps it retain moisture. Using olive oil on your skin creates a layer of linoleic acid that helps to retain the moisture already contained in your skin. Sesame oil also provides this effect. 100% Aloe Vera gel, store bought moisturizers, almond oil, and mineral oil can also help moisturize and protect the skin as well.

Green tea is packed with antioxidants, which reduce the amount of free radical compounds in your body and can help reduce your rate of aging. Try brewing some white tea and then mixing green tea powder into it until a thick paste is formed. Use this as a face mask for twenty minutes, then rinse. You will find that your skin appears plumped, and you will have loaded your skin with a massive dose of antioxidants.

Drinking a cup of ginger tea every morning will load your body with gingerol, which is known to reduce the effects of collagen breakdown. Collagen breakdown reduces the elasticity of your skin and causes the appearance of wrinkles. Sweeten your ginger tea with honey for extra anti-inflammatory benefits. All natural organic raw honey tends to have the most health benefits.

For a more in-depth look at anti-aging and how to take care of your skin, body, and mental health, please check out my books: Anti-Aging Cure and Acne Cure.

Chapter 5: Protecting Your Body With Cardiovascular Exercise

As I mentioned a few chapters ago, cardiovascular exercise, otherwise known as "cardio," is one of the best kinds of exercises you can engage in for overall health. Cardio exercises strengthen your heart and lungs and can help protect you against a number of diseases and ailments. Cardio can cut your risk of heart disease, osteoporosis, and much more. One of the best things about cardio is that there are many different exercises you can do to get a great workout. Cardio exercises include walking, jogging, swimming, running, elliptical cross-training, rowing, biking, jumping rope, hiking, kickboxing, and much more. Many sports, like tennis and basketball, also count as good cardio exercises. It is important to get into the habit of doing cardiovascular exercise as soon as possible if your not already doing it. Heart disease and osteoporosis are no joke and it is important to keep your body as healthy as possible to fend these diseases off.

How Cardio Can Help Your Body

Heart disease can be hereditary and cardio can help you keep your body in tip-top shape to help prevent it from affecting you. Heart disease includes coronary artery disease, arrhythmias, heart failure, cardiomyopathy, angina, and congenital heart disease. Your diet plays a big role in preventing or allowing heart disease to affect your body. Many people believe that the Mediterranean diet is the best way to go when it comes to preventing heart disease. As usual, whole grains, fruits, and vegetables are the best foods to eat to protect your heart. The best types of cardio exercise for preventing heart disease are swimming, walking, biking, running, and internal training. For more information on understanding heart disease and to learn about the best modern medical and all-natural approaches to combating it, please see my book: Heart Disease Cure.

Osteoporosis, a disease that weakens your bones, also affects a large number of the population, but can be combated with plenty of cardio as well. Osteoporosis affects 55% of people over the age of 50, so by getting into the habit of exercising as early in life as possible, you can reduce your chances of developing it. If you do develop osteoporosis, your chances of fracturing your hip, wrist(s), rib(s) and spine can dramatically increase. Your chances of developing osteoporosis vary depending on your age, gender, ethnicity, and medical history. Most often than not, many doctors will not be able to diagnose osteoporosis until it is too late. A diet with plenty of calcium and vitamin D can also help prevent osteoporosis, as long as you avoid lead and mercury. For more information on understanding osteoporosis and to learn about modern medical and all natural ways to treat it, please check out my book: Osteoporosis Cure.

Cardio can also be challenging for smokers, since it works your heart and lungs. Smoking causes harmful chemicals like tar to stick to your lungs, making it harder to breathe over time. It can also cause blood clots to form in your arteries, which can negatively affect your heart. If you're a smoker or if you're planning on quitting, a good cardio exercise to start with is a brisk walk. Not only is a brisk walk healthy for you but it can also help you curve the urge to smoke a cigarette. Once you eventually quit, you can start to get into more intense cardio exercises. However, if you are a smoker, you should seriously consider quitting. It is better for your heart, lungs, and overall health. Not smoking can make you a great role model for your children, friends, and family members. For more information on how to kick the habit, please check out my book: Quit Smoking Now: Quickly and Easily.

Many experts recommend getting in at least 20 minutes of cardio three to four times a week. Anything below that minimum amount will not be as effective. To determine whether you are burning fat, you can calculate it based on your pulse. One good way to do this is to invest in a pulse monitor. Contec Medical Systems makes an effective yet cost-effective pulse monitor.

Best Types of Cardio Exercise

There are three main categories of ways to perform cardio exercises. The first type is low intensity/long duration. During this type of cardio, you can generally take it slow and easy. Good examples of low intensity/long duration cardio are walking or jogging—two great options for beginners. The second type is medium intensity/medium duration. This type of cardio is more intense than low intensity/long duration and it should only last for 20 to 40 minutes. During medium intensity/medium duration, your body can start burning fat and your lungs can improve. The third type is high intensity/short duration. As the name says, this form of cardio should only be performed for 5 to 20 minutes due to its intensity. When performing high intensity/short duration cardio, you should only do it every other day to allow your body to rest.

Next, I will describe some of the other best ways to perform cardio exercises. Some of them are traditional forms of exercising and some of them are a little more fun and exciting. As always, it is important to remember to never over exert yourself, be sure you are stretching and warming up properly and to let your body rest when it needs to.

Mini Trampoline

A Mini Trampoline is a fun and effective way to warm up your body before a workout. I have had one for the last five years and it is always fun to wake up and hop on it for a few minutes to get loose and get the blood flowing before going into my stretching routine. It is also fun to use most any time of the day.

Swimming

Swimming is a great cardio exercise because it is fun and intensive swimming can burn as much as 350 calories in a half hour. Swimming for fun can burn as much as 250 calories in a half hour. If you spend a half hour swimming vigorously and a half hour swimming for fun, you can burn up to 600 calories in an hour. This YouTube video by ACEFitness, Swimming Inspired Workouts, shows a really cool way to create a swimming workout. Swimming is a great way to keep your knees and heart strong.

Outdoor Biking

Bike riding is another fun way to get some cardio in and it's also a great way to work out your lower body. Outdoor biking is more effective than stationary biking because it exposes you to different weather and terrains, giving you a better challenge. One great thing about biking is that you can go fast or slow at your own pace. The amount of calories you can burn while biking depends on your speed and the resistance of your terrain. In general, biking at 10 mph can burn as much as 372 calories and biking over 20 mph can burn over 1,000 calories. This YouTube video, How to Mountain Bike Better by MTBtips, shows some really awesome yet simple workout challenges that you can do with a mountain bike. Biking is a great way to protect your heart against heart disease.

Jumping Rope

Jumping rope even for a few minutes out of your day can do amazing things to your cardiovascular health. This simple workout can positively affect your whole body and as a plus, it helps improve your hand-eye-coordination. You can start out by jumping the traditional way or you can learn to side-step and cross your legs. Jumping rope at a moderate level for an hour can burn as much as 931 calories. Bloom to Fit's YouTube video, 23 Skipping Rope Exercises for a Killer Body, can help give you some really cool jump rope technique ideas.

Jogging

Jogging is a step up from walking and you can do it outside or inside. Like biking, jogging outdoors is better because you can experience different terrains. Start out slow and try to work your way up to jogging at a fairly brisk pace, which is when you can start burning off the most calories. This YouTube video, How to Jog by Livestrong.com, gives some really good pointers for using the proper jogging technique.

Tennis

Tennis is a fun sport to play, you can do it with your friends, and it's a great cardio exercise. It's also beneficial to your body in the sense that it can improve your reaction time, strength, and speed. An intense game of tennis that lasts for an hour can burn between 400 and 600 calories. Check out this YouTube video by Feel Tennis Instruction, How to Play Tennis With Feel, for some great tips and techniques.

Basketball

Basketball is another fun sport to play by yourself or with your friends to get a great cardio workout. Not only does it work your heart and lungs, it can also help you improve your muscles, endurance, and flexibility. Generally, it is possible to burn between 600 and 900 calories if you play an intense game of basketball for an hour. You can play basketball at an indoor court or in your own backyard if you have a hoop and a blacktop.

Hiking

Hiking has so many benefits. It can make you break a sweat, it can improve your muscles, it can burn calories, it can keep your joints lubricated, and it can even combat depression. It's also another fun activity that you can enjoy by yourself or with friends. Some of the best places to hike are in the mountains, Forests, or in State parks or reservoirs. Check your local area for your nearest nature spot. They likely have multiple trails that you can hike on. Hiking is a great way to enjoy nature and clear your mind.

Kickboxing

Kickboxing is famous for being a good source of cardio exercise. It works out your whole body and all of your core muscles. Since you are constantly moving, it can also be a fun workout. You can do this at home or by taking a class, where you might be able to make some new friends. To see some really good beginner's kickboxing techniques, check out this YouTube video by FitnessBlender, Easy on the Knees Kickboxing Blend.

Body Combat

Body combat is a combination of boxing, karate, tai chai, taekwondo, and muay thai. This very energetic cardio workout consists of punching, striking, kicking, and performing other styles of martial arts while listening to music. Body combat can be a very fun way to exercise because it is unlike traditional cardio exercises, such as jumping rope or jogging. To get a good idea of what body combat is like, you can see it in action in Jorgette Joanne Yamyamin's YouTube video Body Combat Cardio with VJ.

Chapter 6: Strength Training

Like cardio, it is important to incorporate strength training into your exercise regime as well. As you age, your muscle mass will naturally decline. However, keeping your muscles strong is important for burning fat, keeping your bones strong, boosting your stamina, managing chronic conditions, and it can even help keep you focused. As you build up your muscles, your body will be able to burn more fat and your bones can become protected from osteoporosis, fractures, and sprains. It can help you stay young as you get old and it can help fend of heart disease and diabetes. Many experts suggest scheduling in two to three strength training sessions a week into your exercise regime, each followed by a day of rest. By engaging in cardio, which burns calories, and strength training, which keeps your muscles strong and toned, your chances of looking and feeling great will be high.

Strength training is really good for preventing knee injuries. Your knees are an important part of your body because they serve as your support system. Your knees can be susceptible to arthritis, cartilage injuries, ligament injuries, and tendon injuries. However, if you keep your knees strong with strength training exercise, you can reduce your risk of damaging or injuring them and avoid having to use braces, wraps, ice packs, or heat therapy to heal them. Some knee injuries require surgery so you can also lower your chances of having to visit the doctor and shell out money for a restorative procedure. Squats, swimming, and lunges can be great for strengthening your knees.

Here are some basic strength training exercises for your knees:

Butt Tucks

Lie on your back and tighten your butt muscles for five seconds. You should repeat this exercise 10 times with a total of three sets.

Terminal Knee Extension

Lie on your back and place a rolled towel under a bent knee. Straighten the knee and hold the position for seven seconds before relaxing. A great YouTube video of the Terminal Knee Extension can be seen here: YouTube Terminal Knee Extension Video.

Quadriceps Contraction

Lie on your stomach and place a rolled towel under the ankle below your injured knee. Push your ankle into the towel while straightening your leg as much as you can while holding it for five seconds.

For a more in-depth look at how to prevent or heal knee injuries, please see my book: Knee Pain Cure.

Another part of your body that can benefit from strength training is your back. Like your knees, your back is another major support system for your body. Back pain can be caused by a pulled or stained muscle or by something more serious, such as a spinal fracture. Preventing back injuries takes a combination of eating right, getting a good night's sleep, not smoking, and exercising your core back muscles, which includes your abs and back muscle. It is also smart to remember when strength training that you need to keep both sides of major muscle groups equally strong or you have a higher chance of injury. For example, Chest/Upper Back, Bicep/Tricep, Quadriceps/Hamstring, and Abdominals/Lower Back. It is wise to try and keep all your muscles strong and not to focus too much on just one area. Yoga strength training exercises are usually the best for strengthening your back against any damage.

Here are some basic strength training exercises for your abdominals and back:

Sit-Ups

Lie on your back and bring your knees towards you with your feet flat on the ground. Use your stomach muscles to bring your upper body up towards your knees. You can put your hands at your ears, hold them up over your head, or put them across your chest. However, don't put them behind your head and pull your head upwards as you do each sit-up, as this can cause strain on the neck. If you need to, place your feet under a heavy object, such as a bed or couch.

Leg Lifts

Lay on your back with both legs straight and together, lift your legs in unison about 6 inches off the ground and hold them for 10 seconds. Then bring them back to the ground and rest. You can do this exercise in sets of 10, or simply hold each lift for as long as possible.

If you want to know all the solutions for back pain, be sure to check out my bestselling book: Back Pain Cure.

Before you dive into the world of strength training, it is important to remember some key tips before you start. Always stretch before doing any kind of exercising and remember to breathe. Even though breathing sounds obvious, some people unconsciously hold their breath, otherwise you may become lightheaded. Try to breathe in during the easy part of the strength training exercise and breathe out when doing the most difficult part. Take strength training slow and allow yourself to rest in between repetitions. Finally, start off easy and don't overdo it—the more you work at it, the more you can eventually get done in a session. If you are more advanced, be careful not to over train, which is a waste of your time and energy. Also, when strength training, it is best to always do 3 sets minimum per exercise that you are doing.

Here are some tools that you can use to enhance your strength training sessions. You can use a stretch band to add resistance to your training, which can help you get stronger. A really good set of stretch bands are these Latex Resistance Exercise Bands. What I like most about this set is that it comes with three different bands for three different levels of resistance. So when you get comfortable with using the easy one, you can move through the medium and hard ones to build more strength.

You can also use a medicine ball to add resistance to your session. Medicine balls are like heavy basketballs and they come in different weights. If you're looking to add a medicine ball to your strength training program, I highly recommend looking into a Valeo Medicine Ball. What I like most about this product is that it comes in different weights. You can choose one that is between 4 lbs and 12 lbs and can be used in the water.

More Strength Training Exercises

Weight lifting is a common type of strength training. Many people are under the misconception that weight lifting is only for body builders but the truth is that anyone can lift weights. There are some very basic weight lifting techniques that you can start out with as you get ready to work your way up. You can perform weight lifting in a gym or in your home gym if you have the proper equipment. I do the majority of my strength training with dumbbells from 10 pounds to 40 pounds. I also have a Bowflex Revolution, but if you want to get into strength training cheaply and effectively, dumbells are a must have. You can exercise nearly every body part very effectively with them.

The first basic weight lifting technique you can try is a **goblet squat**. Start out with a dumbbell that is a comfortable weight for you. While holding it in front of your chest with your elbows pointing down, squat down until your hip crease is underneath your knee crease and your elbows reach the inside of your thighs. To maintain your balance while doing this, let your chest lean slightly forward. Keep your back muscles tight throughout the entire exercise. While in this position use your elbows to slightly stretch out your inner legs. After 20-30 seconds, squat back up again, and repeat 3-5 times. As you learn to master this technique, you can work your way up with heavier dumbbells. For a visual aid on how to do this, check out Phil Scarito's YouTube video Goblet Squat.

Next, you can try a **deadlift**. To do this, stand in front of a barbell that is a comfortable weight. Keeping your back straight, bend your knees and body forward and wrap your hands around the bar, keeping each hand shoulder-width apart. While breathing out, start to pick the bar up while pushing with your legs and bringing your chest up at the same time. Once you have completely picked it up, keep your chest out and bring your shoulder blades back. Bring the bar back down by reversing the process. Once you have placed the barbell back on the floor, you can do another repetition. You can also perform this exercise with a dumbbell. For a visual aid on how to do this, check out this YouTube video, Coaching The Deadlift with Bill Grundler by CrossFit.

Another weightlifting technique to try is the **barbell curve**. This is a good beginner's weight lifting technique. To do the barbell curve, stand and hold a barbell with a shoulder-width grip as you keep your chest out. Keep your elbows close to you and your palms facing forward. Keeping your upper arms stationary, begin to curl the barbell toward you as you exhale. Do this until your biceps are fully contracted. Once in this position, hold it for a minute and squeeze your biceps. While inhaling, slowly return to your starting position. For a visual aid on how to do this, check out Howcast's YouTube video How to Do a Barbell Curl.

For a **single leg dumbbell row**, hold a small to medium sized weight in your left hand and lean forward until your back is straight. For added support you can put your right hand on a chair, bench or other stationary object. Slowly drop your hand holding the dumbbell to the floor and bring one of your legs up until your body is in a T-shape. Next, bring the dumbbell up until it is near your chest. Hold the position for a few seconds and then return it towards the floor. You can do this 15 times for each side for a total of three to five sets. For a visual aid on how to do this, check out this YouTube video, One Arm One Leg Dumbbell Row, by Performance U.

Resistance Band Training

If you're not so much into lifting actual weights you can try resistance band training. This type of strength training allows you to use resistance bands instead of weights, which can save you money on a gym membership or expensive equipment for a home gym. Resistance training is great for building up your bones against osteoporosis.

The first resistance band training exercise you can try is a **lunge with a biceps curl**. To start, simply put your left foot over the band as you position your right foot a couple feet behind you. Grip the handles of your band with your fingers facing up and do a biceps curl and then lunge. You can repeat this 20 times for each leg. For a visual aid on how to do this, check out FITASTIC's YouTube video Standing Lunge to Resistance Band Bicep Curl.

The second resistance band training exercise you can try is a **squat with an overhead press**. To start, step on your band while keeping your feet aligned with your shoulders. With your palms facing away from you, hold the handles of your band at your shoulders. While bringing your arms over your head, squat, and keep your weight on your heels. You can do this 20 times. For a visual aid on how to do this, check out this YouTube video In Motion: Squat to Overhead Press by *Milwaukee Journal Sentinel*.

The third resistance band training exercise you can try is a **side lunge with a side raise**. To start, stand with your feet aligned with your shoulders. Place your left foot over the band, near one of the handles. Using your left hand, hold the other handle. With your right foot, perform a lunge and bring your left hand toward your right foot. Then slowly bring yourself back. You can do this 20 times on each side.

The fourth resistance band exercise is called the **monkey.** To do this, stand with your feet spread out wider than your shoulders. Keeping your knees loose, grip each handle of your band with each hand. While bringing your left arm up, bend your upper body to the right and then quickly do the same with your other side, as if you were moving like a monkey. Do this 20 times for each side.

Yoga Positions for Strength Training

Yoga is a great way to help your body become stronger and more flexible. Anyone can do it, which makes it a great starting point in strength training if you're not already used to lighting weights. Since yoga can help restore your body, you can practice it on the days that you take off from major strength training. It can also strengthen your mind and soul, which is an added bonus.

One great yoga strength training position is the **dolphin plank**. To do this, lie down on your stomach and point your toes on the floor. With your forearms on the ground, pull your abdomen toward your back and raise your hips until you're in a planking position. While inhaling, lift your hips further up until your body is in a V-shape. Hold this position for a few seconds before returning to your starting position. You can do this 15 times in sets of three. For a visual aid on how to do this, check out this YouTube video by Do Your Own Yoga: Dolphin Plank.

A second great yoga strength training position is the **curtsy lunge**. To do this, align your feet with your hips and then, while taking a big step back with your left foot, place it behind your right foot. Bend your knees and extend your left hand toward your right foot. For each side, you can repeat this exercise 15 times in three sets. For a visual aid on how to do this, check out Woman v. Workout's YouTube video Curtsy Lunges for Sexy Legs.

A third great yoga position for strength training is the **Superman** pose. To do this, lay with your stomach on the floor. With your arms and legs extending away from your body, breathe in while raising your arms and legs as high as possible. Hold this position for a few seconds before breathing out and slowly returning to your start position. You can do this 15 times in three sets. For a visual aid on how to do this, check out this YouTube video: Basic Yoga Poses: Yoga: Superman Position by expertvillage.

A fourth great yoga position for strength training is the **triangle.** To do this, keep your feet wide apart and turn your entire right leg 90 degrees while turning your entire left leg 15 degrees. Raise your arms until they are perpendicular with your shoulders. With your palms facing down, inhale and extend your arms and back. While exhaling, turn your upper body to the right, bend down, and place your hand on your lower leg. Be sure to keep your spine straight as you raise your other hand toward the sky. Slowly inhale and return to your starting position. This yoga pose can be a little hard to understand, so for a visual aid, check out this YouTube video, Yoga for Beginners: Triangle Pose, by YoBoFitness before you try it.

My Personal Strength Training Routine

Here is the bodybuilding routine that has been extremely effective for me over the last fifteen years. It is best if you can fit all four workouts into a 8 day period, but at minimum all four workouts should be done in a 14 day period, and then just make your strength training routine a habit and never stop doing it. Ideally you want to take 1 day off after each strength training session. This basic strength training routine has worked great for me, along with a variety of the other exercises mentioned in this book. Also, feel free to mix up the exercises on your own if you are more experienced in order to shock the muscles and stimulate growth.

Leg Day: I will do a short walk around the block to warm up my legs or jump on a mini trampoline to warm up my legs. I will then stretch out my quadriceps, hamstrings, and calf muscles. When properly stretched, I will start off with 25 squats just using my body weight. I go nearly all the way to the ground and I am sure to use good form. I have a Bowflex Revolution, which mimics many of the major exercise machines in a gym. I do light weight leg extensions next to further warm up my legs. After a short rest of a minute or so, then I move on to hamstring curls with light weight and around fifteen or so repetitions. The last exercise will be calf raises. I like to stand on a curb or similar object and just use my calf's to lift up my bodyweight. You want higher repetitions for your calfs, so I will do around 25 repetitions. This completes one full set of all my leg exercises. I then do all these exercises again, only this time; now that I am warmed up, I push myself harder to complete even more repetitions or I will use more weight and fewer repetitions. I will then do at least one more complete set of all these exercises, as 3 is always the minimum amount of sets you want to do. If I feel like pushing myself, then I will do a complete 4th and 5th set as well. The fourth and fifth set is where you will get the most results if you are truly serious about putting on strength and size. If you are going for power and strength, then after the first warm up set, you want to add more weight and lower the repetitions.

Arm Day: On this day I work out my biceps, triceps, forearms, and grip strength. After stretching out my arms, I will take some lightweight, free weight dumbbells and do arm curls with them until I feel nice burn. I will then take an even lighter dumbbell and do my next exercise, which is for the triceps, called tricep kickbacks. The next exercise is for the forearms, and I will do wrist curls with a dumbbell. I then take a grip strength ball and squeeze it in my hands till I got a nice burn. The last exercise is triceps push downs. Near the end of the workout I will typically do a few extra sets of arm curls to really get them strong and looking great. As with all strength training routines, the first set is for warm-up, then you really want to push yourself on the remaining sets.

Chest/Back Day

I start off by stretching my chest and back. I will then take some dumbbells and simulate a bench press motion. When my chest muscles are feeling a bit tired, I end the set with dumbbell flies. I then move to a back exercise, called upright rows. I use a dumbbell with this as well. I will then do another chest exercise called cable crossover on my Bowflex Revolution, and then on to another back exercise called seated rows. I will then do back hyper extensions or planking for my lower back, then some sit-ups, and finish the first complete set with push-ups. Chest back day is typically one of the tougher workouts, but yields great results.

Shoulder Day

I start off by stretching out my shoulders. This routine is done exclusively with lightweight free weight dumbbells. I start the set off with Arnold presses, take a rest, then rear lateral dumbbell raises, then lateral dumbbell raises, and then frontal dumbbell raises. I will then use heavier dumbbells and do shoulder shrugs that work the trapezius muscles. As usual, take a short rest between each exercise.

There a few other things to keep in mind when strength training. You can do your abs and lower back every day, along with your calf's. You can exercise your neck muscles daily as well, and it is good to do various motions with your neck to relieve stress and increase strength. It is also a good idea to eat a protein shake or another healthy food high in protein fifteen to thirty minutes after you have completed your workout. My favorite protein shake is: Muscle Milk.

Concluding Strength Training

Weightlifting, resistance band exercises, and yoga are some great ways to get yourself into strength training. There are many more exercises, moves, and techniques to strength training but this chapter was aimed at helping you become familiar with each category. Try starting out by doing some of the exercises listed in this chapter and then allow yourself to explore and learn more styles of strength training as you get better at it. Life is so much better when you're strong and healthy.

Chapter 7: Vitamins, Minerals, and Supplements

Even though you can't see the inside of your body, know that it's always working very hard! Every day, your blood flows through your body to your brain, your brain sends signals to other parts of your body, and your organs work to keep you alive. These are just some of the everyday functions of your body. However, for your body to work properly, it needs resources. While your body can naturally produce some of the resources it needs to function, you can provide your body with the rest through your diet and supplements. You can do this by eating plenty of foods that are rich in vitamins and minerals and taking a variety of vitamins, minerals, and supplements.

Together, vitamins and minerals can help strengthen your bones, heal your injuries, and boost your immune system. They are also what helps your body convert food into energy and repair damage to cells. If your body goes too long without receiving the proper amount of vitamins and nutrients, it is possible to develop scurvy, blindness, rickets, and other very unpleasant conditions.

Using Supplements

A healthy, balanced diet should be your primary source of vitamins and minerals. However, some peoples' bodies are unable to function properly due to age or other medical factors. For example, pregnant women tend to need extra doses of certain nutrients and seniors' bodies often have trouble absorbing nutrients. Other peoples' bodies sometimes have a general deficiency. In situations like these, it is possible to take a dietary supplement to manually provide your body with the right amount of nutrients. Most vitamins and minerals come in the form of an over-the-counter supplement that you can buy in your local pharmacy, online, or at the local health store. As always, you should always consult with your doctor about any new vitamins, minerals, or supplements you are taking.

I have personally been taking vitamins, minerals and a variety of supplements for the last twenty-five years. While there are all sorts of studies out about vitamins and minerals, I have had an overall good experience with them. When I look around and see other people around my age (just over 40), the difference is quite striking. I look younger, I am much stronger, I still have lightning quick reflexes, my skin looks healthy, I still have incredible mental capabilities, and I possess an overall good physical well-being. Although I'm not a doctor, I think one of the best decisions of my life was to invest in myself, which included a lot of healthy supplements and vitamins over the years. Of course you have to keep up with exercise and strength training as well.

My strategy has been to just give my body all the nutrients it needs in order for it to perform at peak performance. Over time you find out which vitamins and minerals and supplements work best for you, and discontinue taking the items that may not be having the desired effects. My cabinets are filled with vitamins, minerals, and a variety of other healthy supplements that you will see listed in this book. I try not to take too many at one time. I have found that four smaller meals per day works perfect for me, and I usually will take no more than around two to four different supplements after each meal. I have also found it beneficial to take days off from supplementation and to drink lots of water on those days.

Vitamins

Biotin (Vitamin B7)

Biotin is important for your body because it helps your body metabolize fat and carbohydrates. Biotin deficiencies are known to cause skin diseases, nervous system diseases, and intestinal tract diseases because the enzymes in our bodies will not work well without this vitamin. Biotin also helps people who have type 2 diabetes because it helps balance blood glucose levels. Biotin can also help prevent birth defects and can improve the quality of your hair and nails. Although it varies by age and other circumstances, a typical adult body generally needs 30 mcg of biotin a day. Foods that contain biotin include fortified cereal, barley, milk, soy, egg yolks, fish, chicken, broccoli, pork, and spinach. If you need to use a biotin supplement, I highly recommend Natrol Biotin.

Folic Acid (Vitamin B9)

Folic acid is important for your body because it helps promote human growth, it helps our brains and nerves function properly, and it may help reduce your risk of developing heart disease. Folic acid is also known to help protect your body against lung, colon, and cervix cancer. If you are a pregnant woman, you should consult your doctor about increasing your daily intake of folic acid because it can help prevent birth defects as well as improve the growth of your baby. Deficiencies in folic acid can result in memory loss, depression, and cervical problems in women. In general, a typical healthy adult should provide his or her body with 400 mcg of folic acid each day. The best foods to eat for folic acid include green vegetables, beans, fortified orange juice, melons, bananas, mushrooms, and lemons. A really good folic acid supplement is NOW Foods Folic Acid.

Niacin (Vitamin B3)

Niacin is important for your body because it can lower your risk of heart disease by lowering bad cholesterol and increasing your levels of good cholesterol. It can also help prevent asthma attacks, osteoarthritis, and Alzheimer's disease. Deficiencies in Niacin can cause diarrhea, skin diseases, depression, and dementia. A typical healthy adult should get 16 to 18 milligrams of Niacin per day but no more than 35 milligrams. Pregnant women should not provide their bodies with niacin through a supplement. The best foods to eat for niacin include salmon, eggs, leafy greens, tuna, carrots, broccoli, tomatoes, nuts, sweet potatoes, avocados, mushrooms, and whole grains. You can also get Niacin through a supplement. One of the best ones I can recommend is Nature's Bounty Niacin. However, be careful using Niacin through a supplement, as taking too much can cause liver toxicity.

Riboflavin (Vitamin B2)

Riboflavin is important for your body because it helps with your metabolism, energy production, and cell growth. It is also good for helping other B vitamins work properly. Additionally, riboflavin can help protect your body against damaging free radicals. Riboflavin can help prevent jaundice, anemia, memory loss, migraines, depression, and cataracts. Deficiencies in riboflavin can result in cracked skin, sore throats, dermatitis, and general weakness. A typical healthy adult should get between 1.1 and 1.3 milligrams of riboflavin per day. The best foods for providing riboflavin to your body include milk, yogurt, cheese, fortified grains, dark greens, eggs, liver, chicken, fish, and fortified cereals. An excellent riboflavin supplement is Nature's Way Vitamin B2.

Thiamin (Vitamin B1)

Thiamin is important for your body because it helps your body convert food into energy. It is also important for stimulating nerve transmission. Additionally, it can help improve your digestion, metabolism, and muscle functions. Deficiencies in thiamin can result in weakness or, in some extreme cases, even heart failure. The only drawback to thiamin is that your body doesn't store it for long. A typical, healthy adult should get 1.2 milligrams of thiamin per day. The best foods for providing your body with thiamin include beef, beans, pork, enriched pastas, whole grains, wheat germ, bran, nuts, milk, and oranges. One of the best Thiamin supplements is Nature Made Vitamin B-1.

Vitamin B6

Vitamin B6 is important for your body because it helps your brain communicate with the nerves to improve your metabolism and it can also boost your immune system. Vitamin B6 can also help with preventing carpel tunnel syndrome, some forms of arthritis, depression, asthma attacks, kidney stones, and premenstrual syndrome. Deficiencies in vitamin B6 can cause damage to the nerves in your hands and feet. It can also cause dysplasia in women. A typical, healthy adult should get between 1.3 and 1.7 milligrams of vitamin B6 per day. The best foods to eat for vitamin B6 include beans, bananas, cheese, milk, vegetables, sunflower seeds, and fish. A supplement that has worked for me really well is Max Amino Caps with Vitamin B-6.

Vitamin B12

Vitamin B12 is important for your body because it helps create red blood cells and helps maintain nerve cells. Additionally, it helps create DNA and RNA.

Deficiencies in vitamin B12 can cause dizziness, fatigue, oral issues, appetite suppression, diarrhea, and muscle weakness. It can also cause you to develop anemia. Vegetarians and vegans tend to have deficiencies in vitamin B12 because most people get it through animal-based foods. A typical, healthy adult should get 2.6 mcg of vitamin B12 per day. The best foods to eat for vitamin B12 include milk, eggs, cheese, fish, poultry, meat, and shellfish. Vegetarians and vegans can get vitamin B12 in the form of a supplement. I highly recommend trying Jarrow B-12.

Vitamin C

To help your body absorb iron, you should take enough Vitamin C. Vitamin C helps your body repair tissues as well. It also helps protect your body from free radicals and it can also help your body fight off a common cold. Deficiencies in vitamin C can cause aches in your joints and muscles, muscle weakness, and rashes on your leg. A typical healthy adult male needs around 90 milligrams of vitamin C per day and a typical healthy adult female needs approximately 75 milligrams per day. Pregnant women and smokers should consult their doctors about providing their bodies with a higher intake of vitamin C. The best foods to eat for vitamin C include most fruits and vegetables but especially oranges and yellow bell peppers. A really good vitamin C supplement is Nature's Way Vitamin C.

Vitamin A

Vitamin A is important for your body because it helps your bones grow and it also helps improve your immune system and reproductive health. It can also help fend off certain viruses and bacteria and it can help improve your eyesight and vision. Deficiencies in vitamin A can lead to night blindness and it can make certain diseases, such as measles and pneumonia, become fatal. The best food to eat for vitamin A is beef liver. Three ounces of beef liver will provide your body with more than enough of this vitamin. You can also get vitamin A by eating plenty of fruits and vegetables. A very good supplement for vitamin A is Now Vitamin A.

Vitamin D

Vitamin D is important for your body because it helps your body absorb calcium, essentially strengthening your bones. Vitamin D helps reduce your chances of developing osteoporosis, fracturing your bones, and it can even give your immune system a boost. Since the sun can provide us with this vitamin, people who do not get much exposure to sunlight tend to have vitamin D deficiencies. A typical, healthy adult should get 5 mcg of vitamin D each day. The best foods to eat for getting plenty of vitamin D include milk, fortified cereal, tuna, eggs, and salmon. However, it can be challenging to get enough vitamin D in your diet because many foods contain a form of it that the body cannot utilize very well. A really good vitamin D supplement that you can use to heighten your daily intake of vitamin D is Now Foods Vitamin D.

Vitamin E

Vitamin E is important for your body because it helps keep your skeletal muscles strong. It is also known to boost your immune system and help form red blood cells. Although vitamin E deficiencies are rare, common signs of them include defecation issues. Although typical, healthy adult should get 15 milligrams per day, pregnant women should get 19 milligrams per day. The best foods for getting vitamin E include spinach, avocados, whole grains, nuts, wheat germ, and vegetable oils. If you're looking to take a vitamin E supplement, I would suggest checking out Kirkland Signature Vitamin E.

Vitamin K

Vitamin K is important for your body because it helps regulate blood clots, it helps calcium move through you, and it can help decrease your risk of a bone fracture. Deficiencies in vitamin K can lead to osteoporosis as well as gastrointestinal bleeding and bloody urine. A balanced diet should be enough to provide your body with vitamin K. You can get vitamin K by eating leafy greens, Brussels sprouts, wheat bran, and liver. You can also get it by drinking green tea. Fermented dairy and soy products contain vitamin K2, which can also help decrease your chances of fracturing a bone. One of the best supplements that you can take to get vitamin K is Life Extension Super K.

Minerals

Calcium

Calcium is one of the most important minerals for your body. It can help keep your bones and teeth strong and it can help your main organs function properly. It can also help prevent digestive tract cancer, it can help with blood clots, and it can help level out your blood pressure. Additionally, it can help combat food cravings and mood swings as well as helping to relieve premenstrual syndrome. Deficiencies in calcium can lead to a poor appetite, muscle cramps, osteoporosis, and dermatitis. A typical, healthy adult should get between 500 and 600 milligrams of calcium per day. Calcium is prevalent in many foods, so it is easy to get it through your diet. A glass of milk alone can provide you with more than enough calcium for the day. If you decide to provide your body with calcium through dairy products, try to stick with ones that have the words "hormone free" written on the label. You can also get calcium by eating greens, canned sardines, salmon, and broccoli. 100% fruit juices also contain calcium. One calcium supplement that has worked great for me is Vitafusion Calcium.

Magnesium

Magnesium helps prevent the development of type 2 diabetes and heart disease. It can help keep your muscles, bones, and nerves strong. Deficiencies in magnesium can lead to irregular heartbeats, irritability, and muscle weakness. A typical, healthy adult should get between 270 and 400 milligrams of magnesium each day. Foods that contain magnesium include whole grains, avocados, nuts, dark greens, and soybeans. A really good magnesium supplement is <u>Nature Made Calcium Magnesium Zinc</u>. When taking a magnesium supplement, be sure to carefully read the directions, as taking high doses can lead to diarrhea.

Phosphorus

Phosphorus is important for your body because it promotes the growth of your bones and tissues. Phosphorus can also help your body utilize many of the B Vitamins and calcium more effectively. Phosphorus can also help prevent kidney stones and constipation. Deficiencies in phosphorus can lead to muscle weaknesses and, in extreme cases, comas or seizures. A typical, healthy adult should get 700 milligrams of phosphorus each day. Good ways to get phosphorus from your diet are to eat dairy products, including cheese and milk, nuts and pumpkin seeds, peanut butter and peas. A great phosphorus supplement is <u>New Chapter Bone Strength</u>.

Potassium

Potassium is important for your body because it helps your major organs function properly. It also helps with maintaining blood pressure and balancing your fluids. Deficiencies in potassium can lead to weak muscles, changes in mood and an irregular heartbeat. Fruits, specifically bananas, are the best kinds of foods to get Potassium from, but you can also get it by eating potatoes and dark greens. A really good potassium supplement is <u>Potassium Citrate</u>.

Sodium

Sodium is important for you because it helps your body balance its water regulation and digest food. It also helps your circulatory and nerve systems function properly. Additionally, sodium can help your body prevent blood clots and high blood pressure. A typical, healthy adult should get between 1,500 and 2,000 milligrams of sodium per day. Sodium is naturally found in many foods that are part of a healthy diet. Sodium deficiency can get to be a major problem as we get older, so if you ever feel light headed or dizzy and can't figure out why, you may want to have a doctor check your sodium levels.

Chromium

Chromium is important for you because it can help your body store carbohydrates, fats, and proteins, which are important for metabolism. Chromium is also known to help prevent heart disease by raising the levels of "good" cholesterol in your body. Chromium deficiencies can lead to extreme tiredness and type 2 diabetes. A typical healthy adult male should get 35 mcg of chromium each day and women should get 25 mcg. The best foods to eat for chromium include whole grains, meat, broccoli, tomatoes, romaine lettuce, raw onions and fruits. You can also get it by drinking grape juice. If you're looking to take a chromium supplement, I highly recommend Now Foods Chromium.

Copper

Copper is important for your body because it can help red blood cells form, it can help prevent osteoporosis, and it can help your heart and arteries function properly. **Copper deficiencies can cause chronic diarrhea and fatigue.** A typical, healthy adult should get 900 mcg of copper each day. Foods that are great sources of copper include shellfish, vegetables, and whole grains. A great copper supplement is Solaray Zinc Copper.

Fluoride

Fluoride is important for your body because it can help your teeth stay strong, which can reduce the chances that you will develop cavities or experience tooth decay. Fluoride can be so helpful to your oral health that it is added to most public water. Deficiencies in fluoride can lead to tooth problems and if you go a long time without it, it can lead to osteoporosis. A typical, healthy adult should get between 3 and 4 milligrams of fluoride each day. The best way to naturally get fluoride is to drink fluoridated water, although tea can also have fluoride.

Iodine

Iodine is important for your body because it can help your thyroid gland produce essential hormones that help the major organs of your body function. It also helps your thyroid gland regulate your body temperature. Deficiencies in iodine can lead to thyroid gland problems, weight gain, and increased colds. A typical, healthy adult should get 150 mcg of iodine each day. Good foods to eat for iodine include iodized salt (but be careful not to overload on salt. As long as you're eating a healthy diet, you shouldn't need to use it), dairy products, seaweed, fish, and canned tuna. For an iodine supplement, I highly recommend Nature's Way Kelp.

Iron

Iron is important for your body because it helps oxygen travel through your lungs. It also helps your muscles utilize oxygen. Deficiencies in iron can lead to anemia, which is when your body does not have enough levels of hemoglobin. It can also lead to fatigue. A typical, healthy adult should get 8 milligrams of iron each day. Good food sources of iron include soybeans, spinach, lentils, chickpeas, liver, lean ground beef, clams, and oysters. If you want to get iron through a supplement, I highly recommend trying Nature Made Iron.

Manganese

Manganese is important for your body because it can help metabolize fats and carbohydrates as well as stimulate the growth of your bones and connective tissue. It can also help protect your body against free radicals. Additionally, manganese can help protect your body from osteoporosis, arthritis, and diabetes. A typical, healthy adult should get between 1.8 and 2.3 milligrams of manganese each day. The best foods to eat for manganese include pineapple, nuts and seeds, oats, unrefined cereals, and wheat germ. A really effective manganese supplement is Twin Lab Manganese.

Molybdenum

Molybdenum is important for your body because it can help your body break down amino acids and utilize enzymes. Although molybdenum deficiencies are extremely rare, they can result in brain damage if left untreated. A typical, healthy adult should get 45 mcg of molybdenum each day. The best foods to eat for molybdenum are plant-based foods that are grown in the soil, such as peas, lentils, and legumes. You can also get it from leafy vegetables and cereal. A really great molybdenum supplement is Now Foods Nac-Acetyl Cysteine.

Selenium

Selenium is important for your body because it acts as an antioxidant, which can help protect your body against free radicals. It can also help boost your immune system and thyroid gland functions. Additionally, it can help protect you against prostate cancer and heart disease. Deficiencies in selenium can lead to thyroid problems and heart issues. A typical, healthy adult should get between 55 and 70 mcg of selenium each day. Brazilian nuts are the best kind of food to eat for selenium. You can also get it by eating whole grains, garlic, raisins, walnuts, fish, shellfish, and sunflower seeds. For an excellent selenium supplement, I highly recommend Now Foods Selenium.

Zinc

Zinc is important for your body because it can help boost your immune system, it can help preserve your vision, and it can help your wounds heal more quickly. Deficiencies in zinc can lead to skin rashes, weight loss, hair loss, and depression. A typical, healthy adult should get 15 milligrams of zinc each day. Vegetarians should get 30 milligrams of zinc per day. Foods that come from animal sources are excellent ways to get zinc. You can also get it by eating nuts and plant-based foods. A good supplement for zinc is Nature Made Calcium Magnesium Zinc.

Omega-3 Fatty Acids

Omega-3 fatty acids, otherwise known as fish oil, are essential for your diet but your body cannot produce it. Without fatty acids, your body can be susceptible to inflammation, a heart attack, cancer, or rheumatoid arthritis. Deficiencies in omega-3 fatty acids can lead to increased thirst, dry skin, and bladder issues. A typical, healthy adult should eat fish at least twice a week or take an omega-3 supplement. The best kinds of fish to eat for omega-3 fatty acids are oily fishes, such as herring, cod, salmon, and sardines. If you're not a fan of fish, I highly recommend the supplement Nature Made Fish Oil.

Healthy Green Drinks

An excellent way to get premium nutrition into your body is to regularly drink healthy green drinks. These are mostly made from vegetables. You can make your own with a juicer or high performance blender, or you can buy some professional supplements. Wheat grass would be an excellent choice. It is great for energy and overall health. My favorite healthy green drink is Perfect Food Super Green Formula. I have been taking this once or twice a day for several years now and would highly recommend it. It is good for energy and boosting the immune system. I actually went two years straight without getting sick by taking this supplement daily.

Best Combinations of Vitamins and Minerals

Energy

If you want to become more energetic, eating and exercising right is a must. You can also help your body feel better by combining certain vitamins and minerals, which can naturally make you more energized. Be sure to provide yourself with the proper amount of vitamin B12, vitamin B6, folic acid, and niacin. These substances help your body convert food into energy. Iron is also important for staying energized because it helps your bloodstream get enough oxygen.

In addition to vitamins and minerals, there are also some all-natural routes you can go to help yourself stay energized. You can add some of the following supplements into your diet or you can take them with your meals to give yourself an extra boost of energy throughout the day. Becoming more energized can help you become more focused and motivated to keep yourself healthy.

Licorice Root

Licorice root is one of my favorite natural, energizing supplements and has worked great for helping me feel more energized throughout the day. Licorice root helps boost our energy levels by helping our bodies regulate stress-inducing hormones. One licorice root supplement that has worked great for me is **Nature's Way Licorice Root**.

Oat Straw Extract

Oat straw extract is a natural substance that helps your heart pump more blood to your brain. A really good oat straw extract is: **Iowa Select Oatstraw Extract**. It is widely known to be helpful for people wakeup feeling extremely tired in the morning. It comes in liquid form, which is appealing to those who do not like to swallow pills. You can put it in your juice or tea and drink it right down. If you often feel tired in the morning, this product may work well for you. I have noticed a considerable difference in waking up in the morning with more energy once I started taking this product in the morning mixed in with a glass of water. I also take it at night sometimes as it does not keep me awake.

Rhodiola

Rhodiola is a great natural supplement to take if you often find yourself feeling sluggish in the afternoon. This substance helps duplicate the molecules in the body that give us energy. I highly recommend the **NOW Foods Rhodiola Rosea** supplement. Unlike many herbal supplements, this brand does not have a smell or a taste, which makes it easy to take.

Coenzyme Q10

Coenzyme Q10 helps with an energy boost by enhancing the way that energy-producing molecules recharge in our bodies. Although our bodies produce this substance on its own, some people may have deficiencies, such as those with AIDS, heart failure, or high blood pressure. One great coenzyme Q10 supplement is **Nature's Bounty Co Q10.** This product helps support heart health while also giving an extra spurt of energy.

Ginseng

Ginseng is a natural, plant-based herb that grows in Asia and North America. Ginseng is best known for boosting the immune system and lowering sugar levels in the blood. One excellent brand of a natural ginseng supplement is **Irwin Naturals Ginza Plus Endurance**. The key ingredients are omega-3 fatty acids, rhodiola, and ginseng.

Spirulina

Spirulina is a plant that thrives in water and has a texture that is similar to seaweed. Though it is similar to algae, it is actually very healthy for the body and good for energy because spirulina contains high levels of protein. You can take spirulina through a supplement. A great spirulina supplement is **Emerald Energy Defense**. The formula in this supplement promotes good health in general to keep your physical and mental energy levels consistently high. You can stir this substance into a glass of cold milk or juice every morning with breakfast.

Gotu Kola

Gotu Kola is a natural substance that countries like China and India have used to improve mental focus. It comes from a plant and does not contain any caffeine. If you often suffer from stress and anxiety, gotu kola may be able to help you relax and clear the fog from your head. A great way to take gotu kola is to take **Nature's Way Gotu Kola**. It can be taken with breakfast or lunch, depending on when you feel the most sluggish.

For a more in-depth look at how to learn to live an energetic lifestyle, please be sure to check out my book Ultimate Energy. This book can teach you how to make changes in your diet, lifestyle, and sleeping habits to live a happier, more energetic life.

Weight Loss

To help your body lose weight and keep it off, proper diet and exercise is essential. Some vitamins and minerals can help you with this. Calcium, vitamin D, and Omega-3's are the best vitamins and minerals to combine in order to help yourself lose weight. Vitamin D sends signals to your brain to help you stop eating and omega-3's can help reduce emotional-based eating. Calcium can bind to your GI tract, which makes it harder for your bloodstream to absorb fat.

Strength Gain

Many vitamins and minerals are excellent for gaining strength because they support strong bones and muscles. The best vitamins for building strength are vitamin C, vitamin A, all B vitamins, and folic acid. Vitamins can help you boost your endurance, produce more adrenaline, and reduce muscle soreness. A really great way to provide your body with all of these vitamins at once is to eat a balanced diet along with a multivitamin. A multivitamin that has worked really well for me is Opti-Men Multivitamin. There is also a version available for women Opti-Women. The best minerals for gaining strength are manganese, calcium, zinc, magnesium, copper, and iron. Minerals are best for helping you improve your bone strength and helping you stay energized through your workouts.

Chapter 8: Don't Forget Your Mental Health

So far in this book, we've covered almost every way to take care of your physical health, but when it comes to staying healthy; your mental health should be of utmost importance as well. Having a clear, stress-free mind is crucial for being able to stick to your diet and exercise regime, it helps you sleep better at night, can improve self-confidence, and most importantly, it can make you a stronger and happier person. There are so many things to do and see in life, so being healthy and happy is always a good goal to try and achieve on a regular basis. This chapter will cover a few ways that you can take care of your mental health as you begin to get in the practice of dieting and exercising.

Don't Forget To Laugh

At some point in your life, somebody has probably told you that the best medicine is—laughter. I don't know about you, but when I laugh, it sure makes me feel great. Some of the best moments all of us remember throughout our lives are the times when we've laughed our hearts out. Here are some great ways to get some more laughter into your life:

- Read a book, watch TV, play a video game, or do something with other people. Studies have shown that these activities can stimulate a social setting, where laughter is much easier to come by.
- Spend time with children, whether you're babysitting a friend's child or spending time with younger family members. Children tend to laugh more than adults but their laughter can be very contagious.
- Be creative. Make up your own words to your favorite song or try to come up with your own jokes. Creativity is great for stimulating laughter.
- Watch a comedy movie, show, or YouTube video to give yourself a quick laugh.

For more strategies on how to laugh more and how to integrate laughter into your diet, please check out my book <u>Laughter and Humor Therapy</u>.

Get a Massage

A massage is a great way to help your body relax because it focuses on getting rid of any tension in your body. Tension can often be uncomfortable or cause additional pain in other body parts, so it is very important to treat yourself to a massage once in a while. A massage can help you eliminate headaches, improve your skin, fend off sore throats, reduce muscle stiffness, treat digestion problems, treat muscle or joint problems, and much more. You can go get a professional massage, but if you're looking to stay at home and save money, you can easily give yourself your own massage without breaking the bank.

Aromatherapy is also a great tool for creating a relaxing environment anywhere in your house. One way to do this is to invest in an oil diffuser and use different scented oils to stimulate your senses. One product that I can really recommend for this is the Aromatherapy Essential Oil Diffuser. This diffuser is durable, works great, uses water vapor, and you can use it with most essential oils. There are many oils to choose from, depending on what type of mood you're trying to get into. Some of the most popular oils include Peppermint, Lavender, Sandalwood, Cinnamon, and Eucalyptus. You can also invest in a small bottle of massage oil to help reduce the friction between your hands and skin. A really great massage oil is Almond Oil. For body parts that are hard to reach, you can reach them with the help of a foam roller or massage ball.

Massages, aromatherapy, and acupressure, which is another type of massage, is an excellent way to slow aging. To try and combat osteoporosis with aromatherapy, utilize oils such as fennel, rosemary, lavender, marjoram, roman chamomile, black pepper, and benzoin. You can massage them gently into the skin, or add them to warm baths to release the powerful aromas. There are also massage techniques for combating heart disease, back pain, acid reflux, and vision problems. For a more in-depth look at how a massage can benefit every part of your body and treat certain conditions and ailments, please check out my book The Best of Massage Therapy, Trigger Point Therapy, and Acupressure.

A massage can be very beneficial to you if you play a sport, work out a lot, suffer from osteoporosis or any other bone condition, or otherwise put a lot of work on any part of your body. It can also be very beneficial for those who do a lot of typing or computer work. Many people who engage in those two activities can be prone to developing carpel tunnel syndrome, a condition in which the nerves in the end of your wrist get pinched. With painful wrists, it can be hard to exercise, cook, or engage in any other activity that your health relies on. To learn more about preventing carpel tunnel or to learn how to treat it with massages and other techniques, please check out my book Carpel Tunnel Syndrome Solution.

Hypnosis

Sometimes, it can be really hard to make changes in your life, especially if you have been living one way for a long time. One additional way to help yourself overcome fears of changing or to help yourself relax is hypnosis. To get started, you can check out the resources available on HypnosisDownloads. There is help for everything from eating healthy to addiction help (maybe to help you kick your smoking habit) to breaking bad habits to losing weight and more. Here are some helpful titles you may be interested in: Weight Loss, Breaking Bad Habits, Personal Fitness, Relaxation Techniques, Stellar Success, Will Power Booster, and a must have for everyone: Mindful Meditation. Be sure to check out the website for a complete list of options. HypnosisDownloads

Yoga

As you know from the chapter on strength training, yoga is good for building muscles, but it is also good for taking care of your mental health, too. Yoga can ease your mind, allow you to recharge your focus, and it is an overall soothing activity. It is also good for treating specific conditions.

Here are some good yoga poses you may want to try:

The **baddha konasana**. While sitting on the ground, bring the soles of your feet together, and let your knees drop as far towards the ground as you can. Pull your heels in as close to your groin area as possible. Then, wrap your hands around your feet, sit up nice and tall so that your spine is straight, and relax your shoulders. Flutter your knees up and down to loosen your lower area. If you are limber enough, lower your face down to the ground, keeping your hands on your feet and your back straight. Hold the position for 5 to 10 breaths, and then roll yourself back to the upright position, repeating as needed.

The **ardha matsyendrasana**. While sitting on the ground, cross your right foot to the outside of your left thigh. If you don't feel limber enough, place the right foot on the inside of the left thigh. Once you are comfortable, arch your left toes back towards you, so you feel a pull in your left calf area. Then, hook your right arm in front of your right knee, and turn to look back over your left shoulder. Remember to inhale and exhale deeply, and keep your spine straight. Hold for 5 to 10 breaths, and then repeat on the other side.

The **baddha konasana**. While sitting on the ground, bring the soles of your feet together, and let your knees drop as far towards the ground as you can. Pull your heels in as close to your groin area as possible. Then, wrap your hands around your feet, sit up nice and tall so that your spine is straight, and relax your shoulders. Flutter your knees up and down to loosen your lower area. If you are limber enough, lower your face down to the ground, keeping your hands on your feet and your back straight. Hold the position for 5 to 10 breaths, and then roll yourself back to the upright position, repeating as needed.

The **ardha matsyendrasana**. Sitting on the ground, cross your right foot to the outside of your left thigh. If you don't feel limber enough, place the right foot on the inside of the left thigh. Once you are comfortable, arch your left toes back towards you, so you feel a pull in your left calf area. Then, hook your right arm in front of your right knee, and turn to look back over your left shoulder. Remember to inhale and exhale deeply, and keep your spine straight. Hold for 5 to 10 breaths, and then repeat on the other side.

Conclusion

I hope this book was able to help you learn about all the different things that you can do in order to be healthier!

The next step is to make a list of all the healthy strategies you would like to implement into your life. You don't have to do everything at once, but order your list according to priority and then make a strategic goal/plan. Once you have a good strategy in place, it's time to implements it. If you've been wanting to make positive changes in your health and lifestyle, the time to start is now. If you have any questions, be sure to talk to your doctor.

Remember to take your time and don't overwhelm yourself—it takes time, patience, and persistence. Set a personal health goal for yourself and take as many steps as you need to successfully achieve it. Keep track of your progress to help yourself stay motivated and so that you can see how far you have come. You can also try to find a work out partner or enlist your friends to help with encouraging you. Remember, everyone will not be perfect all the time, just do your best and you should see some great results!

Finally, if you discovered at least one thing that has helped you or that you think would be beneficial to someone else, be sure to take a few seconds to easily post a quick positive review. As an author, your positive feedback is desperately needed. Your highly valuable five star reviews are like a river of golden joy flowing through a sunny forest of mighty trees and beautiful flowers! *To do your good deed in making the world a better place by helping others with your valuable insight, just leave a nice review.*

Thanks and Best of Luck

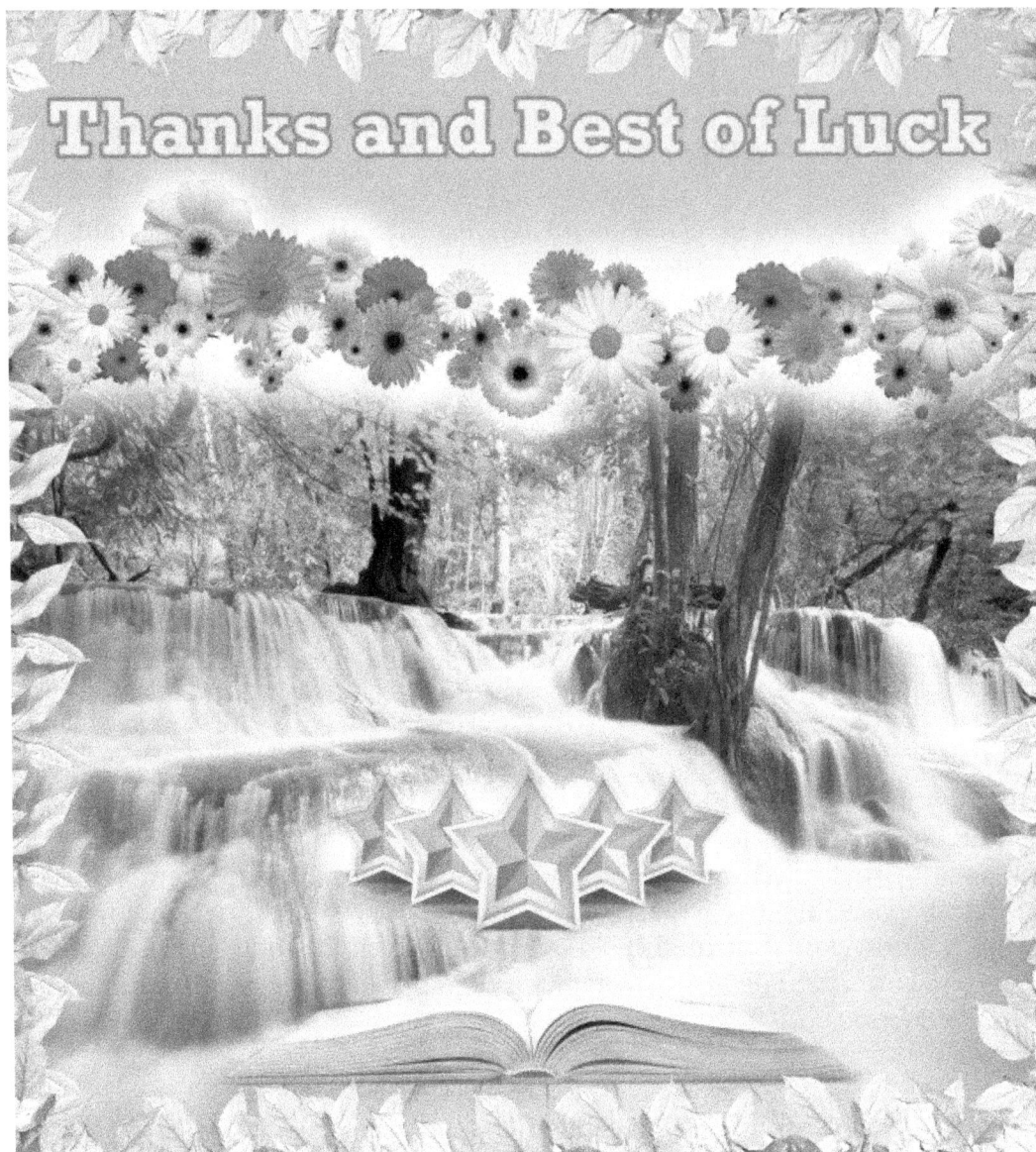

My Other Books and Audio Books
www.AcesEbooks.com

Health Books

ULTIMATE HEALTH SECRETS

HEALTH

Strategies For Dieting, Eating Healthy, Exercising, Losing Weight, The Mediterranean Diet, Strength Training, And All About Vitamins, Minerals, And Supplements

Ace McCloud

ENERGY
ULTIMATE ENERGY

Discover How To Increase Your Energy Levels Using The Best All Natural Foods, Supplements And Strategies For A Life Full Of Abundant Energy

Ace McCloud

RECIPE BOOK

The Best Food Recipes That Are Delicious, Healthy, Great For Energy And Easy To Make

Ace McCloud

MASSAGE THERAPY

TRIGGER POINT THERAPY
ACUPRESSURE THERAPY
Learn The Best Techniques For Optimum Pain Relief And Relaxation

Ace McCloud

LOSE WEIGHT

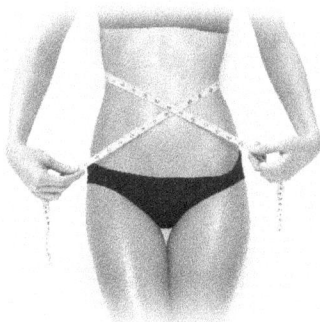

THE TOP 100 BEST WAYS TO LOSE WEIGHT QUICKLY AND HEALTHILY

Ace McCloud

FATIGUE
OVERCOME CHRONIC FATIGUE

Discover How To Energize Your Body & Mind So That You Can Bring The Energy & Passion Back Into Your Life

Ace McCloud

Peak Performance Books

SELF DISCIPLINE

Unleash The Power Of Self Discipline, Influence And Willpower In Your Life To Achieve Anything

Ace McCloud

Competitive Strategies

WINNING STRATEGIES

The Top 100 Best Strategies For Peak Performance During Competitions

Ace McCloud

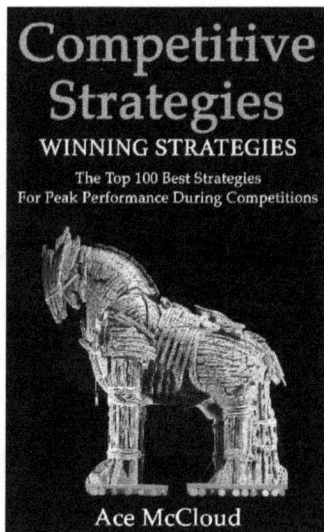

Be sure to check out my audio books as well!

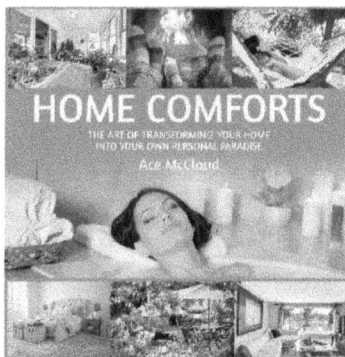

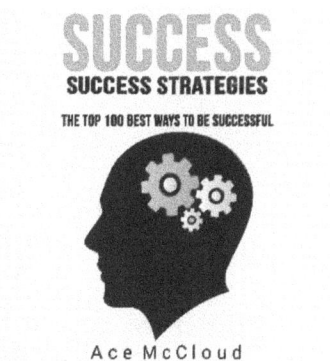

Happiness

The Top 100 Best Ways To Feel Good & Be Happy

Ace McCloud

HOME COMFORTS

THE ART OF TRANSFORMING YOUR HOME INTO YOUR OWN PERSONAL PARADISE

Ace McCloud

MOTIVATION

MASTER THE POWER OF MOTIVATION TO PROPEL YOURSELF TO SUCCESS

Ace McCloud

FACEBOOK

THE TOP 100 BEST WAYS TO USE FACEBOOK FOR BUSINESS, MARKETING & MAKING MONEY

Ace McCloud

HOUSEHOLD HACKS

150+ DO IT YOURSELF HOME IMPROVEMENT & DIY HOUSEHOLD TIPS THAT SAVE TIME & MONEY

Ace McCloud

SUCCESS

SUCCESS STRATEGIES

THE TOP 100 BEST WAYS TO BE SUCCESSFUL

Ace McCloud

Check out my website at: **www.AcesEbooks.com** for a complete list of all of my books and high quality audio books. I enjoy bringing you the best knowledge in the world and wish you the best in using this information to make your journey through life better and more enjoyable! **Best of luck to you!**

www.ingramcontent.com/pod-product-compliance
Lightning Source LLC
Chambersburg PA
CBHW080630030426
42336CB00018B/3141